About Island Press

Since 1984, the nonprofit organization Island Press has been stimulating, shaping, and communicating ideas that are essential for solving environmental problems worldwide. With more than 1,000 titles in print and some 30 new releases each year, we are the nation's leading publisher on environmental issues. We identify innovative thinkers and emerging trends in the environmental field. We work with world-renowned experts and authors to develop cross-disciplinary solutions to environmental challenges.

Island Press designs and executes educational campaigns, in conjunction with our authors, to communicate their critical messages in print, in person, and online using the latest technologies, innovative programs, and the media. Our goal is to reach targeted audiences—scientists, policy makers, environmental advocates, urban planners, the media, and concerned citizens—with information that can be used to create the framework for long-term ecological health and human well-being.

Island Press gratefully acknowledges major support from The Bobolink Foundation, Caldera Foundation, The Curtis and Edith Munson Foundation, The Forrest C. and Frances H. Lattner Foundation, The JPB Foundation, The Kresge Foundation, The Summit Charitable Foundation, Inc., and many other generous organizations and individuals.

The opinions expressed in this book are those of the author(s) and do not necessarily reflect the views of our supporters.

Food Town, USA

Food Town, USA

SEVEN UNLIKELY CITIES THAT ARE

CHANGING THE WAY WE EAT

Mark Winne

ISLANDPRESS

Washington | Covelo | London

Library of Congress Control Number: 2019933782

Keywords: community development, community supported agriculture (CSA), economic development, diversity, equity, farmers market, food bank, food desert, food justice, food security, food systems, sustainable agriculture

You can do lots
If you know
What's around you
No bull
  —William Carlos Williams

Contents

Introduction

The connection between food and place has always fascinated me. When I was a child in New Jersey, the local ice cream parlor run by a third-generation Dutch family forever imprinted on my palate the ethereal pleasures of a chocolate chip cone. As I got a little older, I would ride my bike to the remaining truck farms strung along Route 17. The sight of fresh produce rising out of the dirt riveted my adolescent mind. Years later, propelled by these experiences, I would find myself working as a community food activist in Hartford, Connecticut, where you quickly learned that the world's best cannoli could only be found in the South End (Little Italy).

Food is a big part of any community's identity. But sometimes the cultural and culinary associations of a place can become pigeonholed in the popular imagination. Certainly, when the beginnings of a "food movement" emerged in major cities as well as university and college towns, it was viewed as unique to those places. They were the "bohemian" side of America, where new tastes were formed, innovation was part of the common currency, and quirkiness was an accepted fact of life. Few observers thought that farmers' markets, "real coffee" shops, brewpubs, and artisanal food would make their way to the hinterlands or become a fixture of Main Street America. Even today, many view the food movement—by which I mean the people who are committed to healing the failures of the conventional food system with entirely new ways of producing and distributing food—as a largely urban, wealthy, coastal, and white phenomenon; in other words, elitist.

From my earliest days in the movement, I learned that wealth and a certain degree of sophistication weren't a prerequisite for undertaking food system reform. In the late 1970s, I was placed at the helm of the Hartford Food System, a nonprofit organization in one of the poorest cities in the country. There I was granted the rare opportunity to end-lessly tinker with and even assemble new components of a food system. Though the results sometimes looked like a bad plumbing job, replete with leaky pipes and ruptured joints, the food landscape actually began to show signs of improvement. Gardens abounded, farmers' markets spread like dandelions, and mercifully, drinkable beer and good coffee would "droppeth as the gentle rain from heaven."

At the same time, I was so immersed in my own work that I barely noticed similar changes happening elsewhere. On those few occasions when I'd meet with colleagues from across the state, region, or even the country, I'd be inspired by fellow madmen and madwomen also labor-ing to build a better food system. While most of these people hailed from the larger and more progressive cities, signs indicated that reform was afoot far from my narrowly defined universe. Our smug East and West Coast attitudes would shift from "They couldn't possibly be doing that there!" to "Oh my God! That *is* being done there!"

The food movement was largely action oriented because it was com-posed of activists who over time would spread out across the entire country. As much as I tried to understand the workings of a food system and the interplay of supply and demand, the struggle of capital and labor, I found that, at the end of the day, it was ultimately individuals who drove the change. They are the tinkerers, tailors, and troublemakers turning ideas into projects and dreams into policy.

This book is about the food revolution that is taking place everywhere across America. I've chosen to explore its inner workings by relating the stories of seven cities that are not generally thought of as revolutionary. The food movement has gained momentum and spread to unlikely places such as the ones I describe here. Its influence reached small-town America, rural America, red-state America, and places in America that most Americans have never heard of. While the food movement never issued a formal declaration of war—though industrial agriculture, domestic hunger, climate change, and unhealthy food have mobilized an army of millions in their opposition—it can claim a victory by dint of its omnipresence.

Let's take a brief look at the places my journey took me.

Boise, Idaho: A blue city inside a red-hot state, it may one day become the Portland, Oregon, of the Intermountain West. Boise has a civic and food culture that is progressive but still catching up with the big-name food towns this author has deliberately bypassed. Its most attractive feature is the landscape and the people who love their hometown; its biggest obstacle is the 98 percent of the rest of Idaho that surrounds them. There's a vital local food scene that is gradually bringing farmers, restaurateurs, and food businesses into a virtual group hug, yet there is a hungry industrial food bear roaming the vast countryside, feeding on resources, people, and animals.

Portland, Maine: Like its namesake on the West Coast, the Portland of the Pine Tree State has a robust food culture, more forms of local spirits than a stadium full of drunks could ever consume, and absolutely no space to grow. Its history is rich and salty, its people are as crusty as the crustaceans that have forever defined its food identity, and its civic, nonalcoholic spirit is second to none. Portland is certainly the East Coast's City by the Bay; it is also a refuge for those whom industrial America left behind, and for African immigrants fleeing violence and mayhem.

Alexandria, Louisiana: In the heart of the Deep South, Alexandria is surrounded by cotton fields and pecan orchards, and plagued by a horrific racial history. This Central Louisiana region includes ten parishes (counties) that share some of the worst poverty and food insecurity numbers in the nation, but there's an economic development campaign under way that could also be a model for any place in America. Racial divides and poverty dog Alexandria's struggle to overcome its past; strong collaboration among food organizations and outstanding leadership could make this city the new beacon of the South.

Bethlehem, Pennsylvania: If there were ever an American city that suffered a more crippling body blow from the failures of American industrialism, I don't know where it could be. Bethlehem was placed on life support when the steel industry shut down its blast furnaces, putting thirty thousand people out of work. But its rebound has been nearly as phenomenal as its near-death experience—with food, arts, and entertainment paving the way. A strong connection to the agricultural vitality of the Lehigh Valley is sustained and growing, giving authenticity to many restaurants and food ventures. The benefits of its renaissance are unevenly distributed, however, and its identity is still in flux, but the city's bones are strong, and it has a deep bench of talented instigators and implementers.

Sitka, Alaska: One part *Northern Exposure*, one part rugged individualism, and one part cohesive community, Sitka is both the smallest city in this book and, pound for pound, the most civically engaged. Accessible only by air or water, Sitka is defined by its marine fisheries and breathtaking mountains. The oceans and forests giveth, but climate change may taketh away. Paying some of the highest food prices anywhere in America, Sitkans have banded together to create an array of food production and distribution alternatives. Taking cues from their Native Alaskan community, Sitkans are struggling to share and protect their natural resources as they feel the fiery breath of climate change breathing down their necks.

Youngstown, Ohio: Like Bethlehem, Youngstown was hammered by the shuttering of its steel industry; unlike Bethlehem, Youngstown and the surrounding Mahoning Valley are a long way from recovery. Down to about one-third its former population, the city wrestles with high rates of poverty, a sharp racial divide, too much crime, and an African American infant mortality rate that is one of the worst in the nation. Yet a determined core of young people, most of whom are returning "expats," is using food and farming to revive this once proud place. The Mahoning Valley has been poorly served by Ohio state government, but local institutions—from foundations to hospitals to city hall—are stepping up with a bold rescue plan.

Jacksonville, Florida: Occupying the full boundaries of Duval County in Northeast Florida, Jacksonville is the biggest city in this book. It may be in Florida, but Jacksonville has none of the cachet of Miami or Orlando and still retains the ethos of its naval base and seaport days. Now, more business and corporate than battleships and carriers, Jacksonville has created a food scene that is, in the words of several I interviewed, "just blowing up!" Entrepreneurism and dynamic leaders abound, producing many inspiring food models, but the rising Atlantic Ocean and adjacent waterways conspire to threaten the city's progress. It is a place of swirling contradictions, such as superb small coffee roasters downwind from a stinky Maxwell House Coffee plant, and a vibrant African American food scene largely segregated from the vibrant food scene patronized by white Jacksonvillians.

None of these places fits the standard perception of a foodie city. And just as they are adding new faces to the food movement, so, too, is the movement changing the broader life of these cities. In short, food is becoming critical to their success. For my purposes, "success" refers to a city's quality of life, enhanced by a diverse and exciting food scene, and its ability to take care of its own—in other words, to ensure that *all* are well nourished. (A commitment to addressing the injustices that plague every place is required; the resolution itself takes a lot longer).

It is no wonder that a city's well-being depends on a good food system. The simple activities associated with the acquisition of food not only engender a significant cash flow through a community but also create a nearly infinite number of human interactions. Together, these daily exchanges constitute much of the stuff of community life—food sustains not only our bodies but a large portion of our social and economic existence besides. I shop at the supermarket or the farmers' market; I meet a friend for a cup of coffee and a scone; my children buy lunch at school; senior citizens gather at a congregate meal site; a church conducts a food drive for the local food bank; we garden in our backyards or at a community garden; we go out to a farm-to-table restaurant or local brewpub for dinner, or we gather as neighbors for a Fourth of July barbecue. Food is the tie that binds.

Food's omnipresence, however, often means we take it for granted. For most Americans, food represents a relatively small percentage of their household budget (less than 10 percent), and our hectic lives make food shopping just one more chore we squeeze into our daily routine. That is, until there's a crisis. In late twentieth- and early twenty-first-century America, the crisis sometimes means there's not enough food for some families or, in the case of natural disasters, whole communities, at least on a temporary basis. The crisis can also be gradual, as when the food we eat harms our long-term health or its production damages the environment. The rise in food insecurity, the growth in food banks, and the increase in rates of obesity and diabetes have all conspired to make us considerably more aware of food as both a challenge and an opportunity.

At the community level, where our experience with food is more immediate and where the opportunity for individual action is greatest, Americans have been rallying for decades to fight hunger and unhealthy food choices with everything from food pantries to food business incubators to food policy councils. But less obvious is the way that local campaigns have used food to build and, in numerous places, *re*build communities that have been damaged by socioeconomic forces beyond their control. They've moved from a defensive, "we've got to deal with this crisis" posture to an offensive position that embraces the power of food to drive fundamental change.

Mayors and other elected officials have finally recognized the economic contribution of food, and it has been a long time coming. Throughout my professional life, I have always implored public officials, especially those who can influence policy, to put food on their economic development agenda. Instead of recognizing that a county of 150,000 people generates nearly $1 billion in food-related economic activity each year (I use here the example of Santa Fe County, New Mexico, my home, where the Santa Fe Food Policy Council conducted a local food study), they pursue the pipe dream of a new auto plant or risky dot-com enterprise. Local, state, and regional food assessments, particularly those that examine the economic potential of local food, are nothing new, and are now providing public officials with the data they need. Crossroads Resource Center (crcworks.org), for example, has conducted many economic food studies and has compiled thirty-nine state-level assessments on its website.

In 2016, the United States Department of Agriculture (USDA) and the Federal Reserve Bank of Kansas City documented that local food sales had risen to $6.1 billion nationally in 2012, an astounding increase from $404 million in 1992. This rise is largely a function of increased supermarket, restaurant, and individual household demand for locally grown food, which the USDA now estimates will reach a sales level of $20 billion by 2020. Food industry surveys cited in the report found that 75 percent of all grocery shoppers report consuming local food at least once per month, and 87 percent cite the availability of local food as an important factor in their choice of supermarket. Soaring demand for locally flavored, so-called farm-to-table restaurants has driven expanding economic networks of restaurateurs, chefs, foodies, farmers, brewers, and wine and cider makers.

Beer is one example of how a single item can make an economic difference. While the overall suds market declined by 1.2 percent in 2017 ($111 billion in sales), the craft brew industry grew by 13 percent ($26 billion in sales). American craft breweries now number 5,234. Setting aside differences in taste between craft and conventional beers—an issue that is certainly responsible for more than one barroom brawl—the craft brew industry does several things that conventional beer makers can't do. For instance, one Montana economic-impact study found that the state's sixty-eight craft breweries are responsible for one thousand new jobs, $33 million in additional personal income, and $103 million in additional sales. In Maine, a similarly expanding craft brewery sector provides a demand for Maine-grown grains used to manufacture malt, a necessary ingredient for brewing. The ripple effects haven't stopped with grain production. Some of the state's long-vacant textile mills and shoe factories have been repurposed to provide space for grain drying, which is part of the malt-making process.

Apart from a healthy craft beer market, what are the elements of an effective food movement? In other words, what are the forces, conditions, people, politics, traditions, histories, and organizations that make change happen? Answers to those questions will help cities not only feed themselves well but also diversify their economies, build their climate resilience, and improve their quality of life.

As I made my rounds and conducted my interviews, a number of key elements began to emerge. They are by no means definitive, but the following factors, which play out over the next seven chapters, make a difference:

Communities that pay close attention to the varied economic impacts of food generally do better than those that don't. That being said, none of them give food its full due, but the more food is recognized as an economic engine, the more vital a place becomes.

There's a growing awareness of the importance of food system thinking rather than just individual project thinking. This is not merely an intellectual milestone but also a concept that offers practical benefits as people reach across divides to cooperate. Competition still prevails, but communities that use collaborative competition, or mutual support, are faring better than those that don't.

While it may seem to contradict my last point, I cannot overstate the essential role of the individual. Ideas and actions don't just appear from the "airy nothing"; they are the product of one person, who then seeks out another, then another—until a dream becomes a reality. Entrepreneurism comes in many shapes and sizes, and we see all of them in the food movement.

Obvious as it may seem, a near full spectrum of food activities, businesses, and ideas existed in one form or another in all the places I visited. Yes, fast-food places are still ubiquitous across the nation, but it is far easier to find local food, a craft beer, a food co-op, or even free food than ever before. Quantity and quality varied immensely, of course, but given that many of the places in this book are late bloomers in terms of the food movement, the mere existence of so much choice must be recognized as one big step for humankind.

A revelation for me was the impact that millennials are having on local food systems. (I say "revelation" because I have one of my own, whom I admittedly take for granted sometimes.) But as anyone who has spent time in Brooklyn or Berkeley knows, the presence of younger people has a significant effect on a community. In sufficient numbers, those under forty can become a powerful economic driver, but what was more interesting to me is the number of millennials who are returning to their hometowns in hopes of making a difference in the area's quality of life. Their presence means that change is in the air.

Government also played a role in promoting healthy, sustainable, and equitable food systems. A critical difference among these seven cities was the varying levels and kinds of government involvement. Too much, and the scales of democracy tipped in favor of authority and bureaucracy; too little, and progress was often starved for resources and critical technical support.

Throughout the following stories, I use the phrase "taking care of our own" as a way to lift up the basic principle of good food for all. Sometimes this took the form of ensuring access to locally grown food with the aid of special incentives or bonuses for Supplemental Nutrition Assistance Program (SNAP) recipients; at other times, it was by way of more traditional forms of charity, such as food banks. However it revealed itself, each of the seven cities went to considerable lengths to ensure that no one was left behind.

And lastly, food is not a magic elixir for all that ails America. All the cities I visited were battered and bruised by problems such as failed industries, racism, climate change, opioid addiction, and poverty. Yet the signs were clear that more could be done to use the community-building power of food to address these and other issues.

In each of the seven cities, two basic qualities affect how all the other factors play out on the ground—social capital and compassion. The first term was popularized by the sociologist Robert Putnam, and is based on research that uncovered a decline in social activities and human interaction. This decline is seen in every feature of community life, from how well I know my neighbors to the number of clubs, sports leagues, and civic groups I take part in. By Putnam's measures, social capital has declined between 25 and 50 percent in the United States since the 1960s. The consequences vary from the trivial or even positive (maybe I don't want my obnoxious neighbor knowing much about me) to the highly significant, such as a decline in voting rates. In short, social capital is like a lubricant that can keep a car engine well-maintained and running forever. As I traipsed across the country, it became abundantly clear that food can be a fundamental building block of social capital. Likewise, the absence of social capital makes ensuring that all people are well fed that much harder.

The second quality, compassion, might seem as if it would enjoy more currency coming from the church pulpit than from social scientists. But even the most hard-nosed, data-driven researcher can recognize the importance of basic concern for others. Human compassion has launched literally tens of thousands of food projects—in the United States, mostly in the form of food pantries and food banks. It's safe to say that most of, if not all, these creations were born from empathy, the recognition that I, too, may one day need help. In Peter Block's book *Community: The Structure of Belonging*, compassion is treated as a vital element of community life.

Now, before we proceed further, I must say a word about that term "community": the food movement's most overused word. If I had twenty-five cents for every time I've used it over the course of my fifty-year career, I could have endowed a large foundation capable of eradicating many of the problems I write about. Yet as much as this term is used, we don't often stop to think about what we really mean by it. The definition isn't just an academic exercise. How community is defined has real implications for who makes decisions about a food system and who is affected by those decisions.

Depending on who is using the term and how they're using it, "community" can mean everybody—sometimes even the flora and fauna, the air and water—found within any loosely defined boundary, or it can mean a very select group with a carefully circumscribed set of traits. It can be inclusive, as in, "We want *everyone* in our community at the table," but it can also be used to exclude others, as in, "This is *our community*, and *you* are not welcome here."

To better understand the meaning of community in the places I've visited, I'm relying on two psychologists, David W. McMillan and David M. Chavis, who have identified its four key elements. They are membership, best represented by a feeling of belonging; influence, in the sense of membership making a difference or mattering to a group; reinforcement, by which we mean that participation will also enable the person's needs to be met; and shared emotional connection, as expressed through a shared history, common places, time together, and similar experiences (as presented in the *New York Times Magazine*, "Group Think," April 22, 2018).

McMillan and Chavis further differentiate community into two types, those that are geographic (city, neighborhood), and those that are relational (the connections between people). Without a doubt, the seven cities I visited are defined by specific geographic, political, and sometimes natural boundaries, such as rivers, oceans, and mountains. These physical features are by no means inconsequential, because they influence the performance of the food system. But the communities I visited are also defined by relationships. In other words, the people involved in these seven food systems often know one another or at least know *of* one another; they work together, even if only occasionally; and they have common goals—not always in perfect alignment—unique to their shared place.

These people are in many ways my coauthors. During the course of my travels over eighteen months, I interviewed a total of ninety-two individuals who had a strong stake in their local food system. With the exception of a few people, all those interviews were conducted at length, face-to-face, and often on multiple occasions. These interviews were complemented by background research on all the relevant cities, organizations, and institutions.

With respect to point of view, I have attempted to limit my editorial comments and let people speak for themselves. Of course, no reporter is completely neutral, for no other reason than we must make a judgment call about what we put in and what we leave out of a story. To those who may feel slighted, I apologize in advance. Please know that every word you uttered, whether it appears in these pages or not, informed the totality of this book. My task was to capture the essence, the point upon which other things pivot, and the pad from which they are launched. Those moments often occurred when the person who generously granted me their time became most passionate, when perspiration beaded up on their brow, or when their knuckles turned white from tightening their grip on a steering wheel. That is when we are most revealing; that is when we are most instructive.

Before we turn to those revelations, let me offer a few words about what this book is *not*. First, it is not a manual designed for the practitioner who wants to replicate a food project. Lessons can be learned, of course, and I hope they will, but they are taught herein through stories rather than as a how-to worksheet. Most assuredly, this book is not a puff piece about the wonders and beauty of community food systems, nor is it packed with politically correct platitudes. Similarly, it is not a diatribe against the evils of the industrial food system, which I fully acknowledge are many, and whose effects were often evident in the places I visited. But in the spirit of letting people talk for themselves, I tried to stay true to representing their viewpoints. By no means does that imply that I ignored the problems I saw, or ones overlooked by the interviewees. Divides, failures, and in some cases, open wounds are revealed, and when it made sense, I offered constructive criticism. You will read about the good, the bad, and the real.

This book is not just about food. As I have said many times elsewhere, food is about social change, community economic development, empowerment of citizens and stakeholders, health, climate change, equity, and race. Food is a gateway that I invite you to walk through, not simply for your own satiety but to make a powerful and necessary difference.

CHAPTER 1
Bethlehem, Pennsylvania

I'm gazing out the passenger window of Olga Negron's car at the most sprawling complex of warehouses I've ever seen. Devoid of any signs of human life, hundreds of acres of land are scraped flat as a pancake for giant, windowless buildings stocked full of merchandise for Amazon, Walmart, and Reeb, to name just some of the more prominent brands. The area, known to logistics wizards as LV Industrial Park VII, has roads wide enough to handle eighteen-wheelers running four abreast, which makes Olga's SUV feel like a toy.

This is the landscape of the new American economy, where no one makes anything anymore, but they sure do buy! We're in eastern Pennsylvania, only a few minutes from the New Jersey border and barely an hour from Port Newark, where thousands of containers of non-American-made stuff lands every day. From there, containers are loaded on trucks, which take them to Bethlehem, their temporary resting place until a signal from Arkansas or Silicon Valley directs them to a Walmart in Baton Rouge or a warehouse in Texas. The good society turned into the *goods* society, and in the case of Bethlehem, Pennsylvania, it stands on the ruins of the industrial society. If you dig a few feet beneath LV (Lehigh Valley)

Industrial Park VII, you will find the remnants of Bethlehem Steel, once the citadel of this nation's industrial prowess.

"This is the largest brownfield site in the country," Olga tells me. When she's not serving as the first Latina elected to the Bethlehem City Council, she works for a law firm managing hundreds of personal injury claims. Her clients are Lehigh Valley residents, many of them warehouse workers and 80 percent of whom are Latino. "Warehouse jobs aren't great, but better to build warehouses on brownfields than farmland," she says with the hint of a sigh, one that presaged other sighs I'd hear during my time in Bethlehem. It's a sound like a blues song, one that if you could write lyrics for might go like this: "There were good times, there were bad times / But today's times ain't as good as the good times / Ain't as bad as the bad times."

For more than one hundred years, Bethlehem Steel sprawled across sixteen hundred acres in Bethlehem, Pennsylvania. Its beating heart was a series of belching smokestacks and blast furnaces that forged billions of tons of steel to build, among other things, 1,100 World War II warships. Bethlehem Steel closed in 1995, a victim of a changing world economy, throwing thirty thousand people out of work and terminating the hopes of generations of families that could make solid middle-class lives from good-paying union jobs. The industrial site remained vacant for many years, holding groundwater contaminated with polycyclic aromatic hydrocarbons, trichloroethylene, and tetrachloroethane. Great truckloads of soil had to be hauled away to landfills so that Bethlehem could begin to reinvent itself and create a new identity.

Olga's vehicle wound its way out of Warehouse World into the city's nearby core. We soon passed Sands Casino, which was the vanguard of Bethlehem's post-steel redevelopment—gaming being a tried-and-true government economic-revitalization strategy that too often defines the limits of the public sector's imagination. In the case of the Sands, however, a flickering flame of originality turned into a soft, warm glow of creativity. Yes, it brought roulette wheels to a city formerly powered by waterwheels, but in an uncommon flight of fancy, the casino's developers would preserve the skeletal remains of Big Steel: smokestacks and boilers, massive I-beam sculptures, and giant, ancient gears more reminiscent of the Stone Age than the industrial age. Bold architectural acts of adaptive reuse turned irreplaceable masonry structures into art spaces and museums. In the nineteenth and twentieth centuries, immigrants traveled across the globe to become steelworkers in Bethlehem, each day walking from densely packed neighborhoods to the mill. Today's residents and visitors can still experience an authentic twenty-first-century version of the city's gritty past, generally free of Disneyfication and insincerity.

The casino would not only celebrate the arts but also become the first place in Bethlehem to embrace the country's growing love affair with food. Chef Emeril Lagasse of New Orleans fame would open his first of three restaurants in 2009 in the casino and its adjoining hotel. It was certainly a coup for a city of seventy-four thousand to be the only place in the Northeast with Lagasse restaurants.

Bethlehem would follow a trajectory from mills to warehouses to casinos to arts to food—never a straight line, of course, but certainly a lifeline for a community cast adrift by the sinking of Big Steel. Other forces would contribute as well, such as the city's long-standing academic institutions, Lehigh University and Moravian College; its major hospital, St. Luke's; and in an ironic twist of history, the terrorist attack of September 11, 2001, on the World Trade Center. Barely within commuting distance of New York City, the Lehigh Valley became a refuge for thousands who believed that the metro New York region now had a giant target on its back for fanatics of all stripes. Following 9/11, Bethlehem itself experienced its biggest population bump since 1950.

Brew Works

As one who came to Bethlehem twenty-five years ago from Puerto Rico, Olga takes Bethlehem's renaissance with a grain of salt. "It's still too controlled by special interests, money, and good ole boy politics," she says. While acknowledging the big players who hit economic development home runs, Olga puts more stock in the hundreds of singles that its residents scattered north and south, east and west. These grassroots efforts have created dozens of restaurants, a new Charter Arts high school, a food and farm program at the community college, a new supermarket in a food desert, farmers' markets, festivals, and numerous no-profit and nonprofit organizations that raised the city's quality of life while also taking care of those left behind.

You get a quick idea of what these connections look like while chomping on a Brewers' Grain-Fed Burger at Fegley's Brew Works. It's a half-pound, intense beef experience from a cow raised at nearby Koehler Farms and fattened on spent grain from the Susquehanna Brewing Company. Not only does it take your palate to those special places only a superior burger can go, but its sheer righteousness envelops you in a virtuous glow of sustainability. As I'm washing it down with a Hop'solutely Triple India Pale Ale in one of those oh-so-warm-and-cozy wooden booths, I'm joined by Rich and Diane Fegley, owners, operators, and inventors of Fegley's Brew Works.

"I went to Drexel University for an English degree, and worked for the Johnson and Johnson Corporation, but it wasn't until I got into home brewing that I got interested in the restaurant business," Rich tells me as he unravels the Brew Works creation story. After a stint in Boulder, he and Diane returned to Bethlehem, their hometown and still home to their extended families. They were determined to open a restaurant and brewery, which they did at what was the absolute nadir of Bethlehem's post–World War II existence. "The Bethlehem Steel plant had been slowly shutting down for years . . . and the downtown had been bled by the malls and box stores. On the same day in 1998 when we opened our doors on Main and Broad, the Historic Hotel Bethlehem [just down the street] declared bankruptcy and closed." Rich and Diane were either the most courageous and committed citizens of their generation, or Pennsylvania's most foolish entrepreneurs.

For a couple of years, their restaurant and brewery was a lonely outpost in what decades earlier had been the city's commercial hub. However, their bet—clearly a long shot at the time—paid off, but most important, their business gave heart to others who hoped that downtown, and the city as a whole, would turn around. And it did. Historic Bethlehem, with the Moravian Book Shop as the country's oldest bookstore, proved too strong a draw, and the Historic Hotel Bethlehem would be renovated and returned to its past glory.

As I walked the two blocks down Main Street from the Brew Works to the Hotel Bethlehem, I counted no less than twelve eateries, including a cidery and Johnny's Bagels & Deli. As a bagel devotee, I visited Johnny's the following morning, where I would discover that Johnny Zohir learned his bagel-making craft in New York City. The bagel, cream cheese, lox, and capers were perfectly proportioned and gave me just the right amount of "crunch and chew." The counter help calls you "boss" in that make-believe deferential kind of way until you pay your bill, after which they ignore you completely. They, too, had just the right amount of crunch and chew.

For their part, the Fegleys are committed to sustainability and a more expansive definition of "local." In addition to recycling brewer's grains through livestock feed, they work to reduce waste, including recently eliminating plastic straws, and are active composters. "'Local' is problematic because you can't get enough local," Rich tells me. He also notes that the big food service companies like Sysco and US Foods are certainly offering more sustainable food but no locally produced food. "But with their technology and online purchasing systems, they sure do make it convenient," he notes. Nevertheless, when Brew Works is not buying from farmers like Koehler Farms or Breakaway Farms and Butchery, they are using regional distributors like Pocono ProFoods. By keeping their purchasing and overall orientation regional, Rich and Diane see their business having a significant economic impact. They opened a second restaurant in nearby Allentown in 2007, and altogether the two sites employ almost two hundred full- and part-time staff members. Brew Works inspired dozens of other food and beverage entrepreneurs, and pioneered Bethlehem into a twenty-first-century food scene.

A River Runs Through It

Anyone who knows Bethlehem will probably acknowledge that it is two cities in one, divided north to south by the Lehigh River and seven sets of railroad tracks. The North Side, which includes the historic downtown, most of the higher-end restaurants, and Moravian College, is generally more affluent. Crossing the river over the Fahy Bridge drops you into a cityscape so dramatically different you feel as though a stage manager just pulled a set change on you. While the north's European roots stretch back 275 years, the South Side's are more recent, multiethnic, and blue-collar. Its various neighborhoods, admirably rich in history, diversity, and food, in some ways stand apart from each other, and in other ways are joined at the hip.

Like all writers who want to "do justice" to a place and its people, I struggle to find the voices that can not only tell their story but also relate it to that of their community. That search is never easy, but on really good days—coasting your bike downhill with a strong wind at your back—someone just right falls into your lap. For me, that person was Jake Hoffman, born and raised in Bethlehem and now living in

Portland, Maine, which for the purposes of this book only, means he has "dual citizenship." In all cases, I selected the cities for this book before I selected the people to interview, but when I told my son that I had selected Bethlehem, he reminded me that his four-year college roommate and longtime bandmate, Jake Hoffman, was from Bethlehem. "And he's a foodie, Dad."

Jake, age thirty-three, graduated from Bethlehem's Freedom High School, the city's sister high school to, believe it or not, Liberty High School. His dad worked as an accountant at Bethlehem Steel until it crashed and burned, and then he transitioned to become a railroad engineer. His mother is a high school dance instructor at Charter Arts. When it comes to the divide between Bethlehem's north and south, you might say Jake has dual citizenship there as well. Raised in a pleasant middle-class neighborhood on the North Side, he developed an early passion for food. It's a passion he shares with his brother Eric, who went on to become a professional chef. "Our family always came together around food, which was a time we'd all get creative," he tells me. "Local and fresh food was just kind of a value we grew up with." Though Jake ultimately chose music as a career, his heart and soul are closely linked to food. "I'm the head chef and gardener in our household," he says of the home he shares with his wife, Emily, in Portland, Maine.

Jake's first job as a teenager was at a Thai restaurant on Bethlehem's South Side. "I was fascinated by diversity, so working at the restaurant in that neighborhood gave me a chance to experience it firsthand. . . . The steelworkers were diverse, and so was the neighborhood." There was a strong Latino influence to the South Side's restaurant scene that reflected the influx of people from Puerto Rico, El Salvador, and Peru. According to Jake, none of the restaurants are "super fancy places, but there's enough going on in different neighborhoods to give you a good comparison." Indeed, the Community Action Development Corporation of

Bethlehem lists fifty-one eateries, cafés, wine bars, and brewpubs on the South Side, a rather incredible number given the compressed geography and relatively small resident population.

About the time Jake was heading off to college in 2003, "the food scene just kind of exploded. There were farmers' markets and CSAs. There was also a Wegmans supermarket that opened." Given the chain's reputation for high-quality, sustainable fare, and the absence of a Whole Foods, the arrival of a Wegmans within the city's limits was a momentous occasion. Jake thinks the city's proximity to both Pennsylvania Dutch Country and Emmaus, Pennsylvania, also played a role in its evolving foodie culture. (As one who was subjected to a steady regimen of fatty meat, potatoes, and delicious pies, I would probably recommend that Pennsylvania Dutch cuisine carry a surgeon general's warning.) On the other end of the spectrum, Emmaus is home to the epicenter of America's organic movement, Rodale Press. "Though they may be weirdos, they have had a major influence," said Jake.

When I asked him to compare Bethlehem's food consciousness to that of Portland, Maine, a place he is intimately familiar with, he said with a smile, "Bethlehem's foodies recognize ingredients and seasonality; Portland's foodies recognize their exact location and politics." Wherever Jake's city of residence, his love of food is rivaled only by his devotion to music. "Musikfest defines Bethlehem's identity because it's about food and art!"

Eventually operating on a scale that would dwarf Woodstock, Musikfest started in 1984, featuring 295 performances on six stages, attracting more than 180,000 people to Historic Bethlehem. Over the past three decades, the event evolved into one of the largest and most diverse music festivals in the nation, with more than five hundred shows on sixteen stages over ten days. Each year more than nine hundred thousand people make their way to the Lehigh Valley to experience all the music and food the festival has to offer.

As much as "the food scene has blossomed in Bethlehem," Diane LaBelle says, "it's the arts that saved the city." LaBelle is director and cofounder of the Lehigh Valley Charter High School for the Arts, which opened in 2013. She deliberately chose to locate the school on Bethlehem's South Side, in a redevelopment area that qualified for the federal New Markets Tax Credit Program. The school has 650 students but no cafeteria, which according to LaBelle, is partly by design. She told me that she wants the school to be an integral and supportive member of the community. That means all those students must find lunch off school grounds. Similarly, the school offers ninety-two evening student performances per year that are attended by friends and family members who often use the occasion to dine at South Side restaurants.

Charter Arts isn't the only educational institution in the area. From the South Side's river valley, you ascend quickly to the mountainous heights that envelop 150-year-old Lehigh University. Lehigh is an old institution that until recently maintained a guarded relationship between its campus and the community. When it finally began doing some outreach—breaking through classic town/gown paranoia—a pent-up dam of economic demand flooded nearby neighborhoods. But regardless of timing and intention, both schools are now vital contributors to Bethlehem's South Side food scene.

For its part, Charter Arts draws students from twelve surrounding counties and forty-seven school districts. In Diane's estimation, the arts are a growing field—an industry of its own making—that her kids will move into for decades to come. But having said that, she also describes how food is integrated into the school's life and curriculum. "Food is a big part of the language curriculum, and soon we will have a professional kitchen," I was told when I spoke briefly to a creative writing class during my visit. But for the meantime, the lack of a cafeteria remains problematic, especially since 35 percent of the school's students are eligible for the free and reduced-price federal lunch program. Because there's the economic impact from students buying lunch locally—650 students multiplied by five dollars a day—in a community that still needs more money flowing through it, the school will offer only limited eat-in options for the foreseeable future.

Above and beyond what happens within the school building, Diane maintains that the school's presence is a community magnet that has drawn many new businesses to the immediate area. Her examples are interesting because none of them—a brewpub, a distillery, and a mead-ery (where wine is produced from honey)—could be legally frequented by her kids, but school's existence as a large institution with eating and drinking parents and faculty, combined with thousands of semi-legal drinking Lehigh students up the hill, leverages investment by all kinds of food and beverage interests.

Perhaps most interesting among these start-ups is an emerging food business incubator called The Factory, which just happens to be immediately across the street from Charter Arts. I noticed the building, labeled in the prosaic style of industrial-age America as BETHLEHEM STEEL BUILDING #96, on my way into the school. After getting ahold of the owner, Richard Thompson, I learn that he and his investors are renovating this circa 1950 building into a full-service start-up facility, scheduled to open for fifteen to twenty food businesses in 2019. He describes it as a "millennial innovation center with a Boulder or Austin affect," referring, I guess, to something very hip.

Based on his background, Richard seems like the kind of guy who can pull this off. He was the brains and driving force behind Freshpet, a company that successfully channeled America's hunger for healthy yum-mies for Fluffy and Muffy, and found its way into places like Walmart and Whole Foods. "I made some money when I sold the company," he tells me—"some money" being enough to leverage $250 million of investment in this forty-thousand-square-foot former steel warehouse. He tells me the site itself was very inexpensive but took three months and presumably lots of cash to "clean up and detoxify." He prefers to call the area around him a "greenfield site" rather than the less-cool, federally designated "brownfield site."

Referring frequently to The Factory as a "fun, interesting millennial place," Richard plans to employ thirty to forty people to provide the start-ups with investment, marketing, human resources, food safety, and other "back-end services." So far, the preliminary lineup of businesses includes Mikey's Muffins (baked goods), Belgian Boys (Euro cookie and candy products), Skinny Salamis ("better than jerky"), and Honey Stinger ("honey, not sugar"). In the process of reviewing product lists for these companies, I noticed my cholesterol and insulin levels beginning to rise, but according to Richard, the companies will be ones that make "better, healthier food, even if it's only *less* sugar."

Apparently, Richard could have taken this idea anywhere but chose Bethlehem specifically because it *did not* have an innovation center. He also cites the synergistic connection to Lehigh as well as Northampton Community College and its culinary training program as distinct advantages. Clearly, the presence of a well-financed food incubator in Lehigh Valley adds significant value to its food system, in terms of not just economic growth but more diversified food options too.

That there is a synergy between food and art, built on the ruins of steel, seems like the fairest way to resolve the question of which one has contributed the most to Bethlehem's revival. One without the other would likely have led to very mediocre results all around. But what's still unresolved is the issue of social justice. As the area with the highest poverty rates and most people of color, the South Side is not treated equitably by the retail food system.

I'm having a cup of coffee with Javier Toro at the Lit café, where we are surrounded by dozens of Charter Arts students doing their best to assist the local economy. A member of the Bethlehem Food Co-Op board of directors—a co-op without a business location or significant dues-paying membership yet—Javier is explaining to me why Bethlehem needs a food co-op and why the South Side is a food desert.

The simplest explanation, according to Javier, is that, "the marketplace doesn't respond with good food." He acknowledges that the neighborhood has many bodegas and corner stores, but it is served by only two medium-sized grocery stores. One is called Ahart's Market, which I toured and left as soon as I could. It was a mess, small, poorly lit, and retained the odor of thousand-year-old objects excavated from peat bogs. Reviews on Yelp and similar sites confirmed my impressions. The second store, however, was a C-Town Supermarket on Third Street that opened about three years ago, with the help of some public financing. While still small by current standards, it was clean, well-lit, and stocked with good selections of perishable food items. It also offers a delivery service: a godsend for many of the area's seniors. C-Towns are independently owned franchises widely prevalent throughout the Northeast, especially in urban areas. Online reviews as well as comments from others I interviewed generally gave this C-Town high marks.

Javier, however, doesn't feel that the C-Town adequately resolves the community's need for good food, especially food that is preferred by Bethlehem's Caribbean people, such as Puerto Ricans. Hispanics make up 30 percent of Bethlehem's population, and he reminds me that they have higher rates of diabetes. "Overall, our community's health is not good—too much fried food, sugar, and salt." Jokingly, he adds, "We Puerto Ricans can lose our Spanish in two generations, but we never lose our eating habits, which aren't always healthy!"

The question of whether or not C-Town—or any other supermarket, for that matter—turns a food desert into a food oasis pivots on Javier's use of the phrase "good food." The definition of "good" is perhaps more subjective than "healthy and affordable," a goal that probably everyone agrees is worth achieving. It's not that residents or community leaders challenge C-Town's ability to meet basic food needs; it's that Javier and the five hundred households that have made a preliminary commitment to the co-op have set the bar higher. "Good enough" is not good enough in the eyes of those who now want the best, and given that Bethlehem's South Side is a five-mile crosstown drive to the Wegmans, a co-op food store in or near the South Side just might be the ticket.

But there's something else at stake that Javier describes with passion, and that's the tradition of cooperation and the way it empowers traditionally underserved people. "Puerto Rico has a long history of co-ops," Javier tells me, and perhaps even more relevant to Bethlehem is the fact that cooperation is a local ethic that grew out of its centuries-old diversity. "The history of Bethlehem is based on cooperation. People came here from so many different places to work in the steel mills that they had to learn how to cooperate, or they never would have made it."

As of this writing, the Bethlehem Food Co-Op has launched a membership campaign with a target of three hundred dues-paying members ($300 per household, payable in monthly installments of $25). Once that target is reached, the board of directors will commence the search for a storefront location. The co-op has an active online presence, a qualified board of directors, and a thoughtful development plan.

Northampton Community College

If Charter Arts is the Lehigh Valley's training ground for future artists, the Northampton Community College is the training ground for its future foodies, farmers, and culinary professionals. Spread out across Bethlehem's exurban northern fringe, where the remnants of Lehigh Valley farmland wait their turn for cul-de-sacs and aboveground swimming pools, the community college's campus occupies a substantial tract of land. Part of its expansiveness is, as Pennsylvania's only residential community college, meant to cater to up to ten thousand students. Another reason for its outsize footprint is NCC's East Forty Acre Farm, located on the campus's eastern edge, which is fast becoming a booming outdoor classroom and food production facility.

It's a sunny but chilly April morning that finds me stumbling over soggy turf and dodging woodchuck holes in an attempt to keep up with the long-legged Kelly Allen. He's an English professor at NCC but also the inspiration behind East Forty Acre Farm and the school's emerging food study programs. We're on a tour of the farm, which is about a quarter mile from the center of the campus, but by the time I'm done huffing and puffing my way around the whole farm, it feels like a lot more than forty acres. Currently, Kelly and his program are actively using about 4.5 acres of the land for various garden beds, cold frames, high-tunnel greenhouses, beehives, compost bins, and even a wood-fired kiln—because the arts just can't be too far behind where food is present. A large section of farm includes a wooded portion and open fields that Kelly wants to maintain for wildlife. An additional seven acres that adjoins their production field will be leased to a young local farmer for vegetable and herb production. And to bring along the surrounding, nonacademic community, the farm includes twenty-four community garden beds.

"This land is owned by NCC, but for a long time, all they did was put down weed and feed and cut the grass twice a year," Kelly said. The place was in bad condition, and the soil nutrients were depleted. He tells a story that he now takes as an omen for the school's active use of the land. "I saw a mangy fox out here just before we started work; its coat was missing fur and it was clearly undernourished. After a year of restoring the land, I saw the same fox again, but this time its coat and body were full, and its eyes were bright." Clearly the community college's students saw it the same way. What Kelly thought would be a three-year process to get the land ready and the farm up and running took only eight months because enthusiasm for the place and the program was so high. Today, about 150 students participate in various ways throughout the school year, which includes some paid student summer staff.

Unlike most professions I've encountered, food system work seems to attract people with a personal story that often illuminates their choice of career. Kelly's story is no different, though perhaps surprisingly dramatic. He came from a poor family in Western Pennsylvania, where all the mills had shut down and unemployment was high. His father had a drinking problem and his mother needed food stamps in order to feed the family. Kelly took up hunting, not for recreation but as a way to help put food on the table. "I never forgot being poor. When I met my wife, we started homesteading, and through gardening I came back to food." His attitude shifted from one of scarcity to one of abundance, something that's easily detectable when you listen to the animated way he describes the past, present, and future efforts of the farm and the school's proposed food studies program.

"Food is a means of experiential learning," is how Kelly described the farm's purpose. But East Forty Farm's success has clearly made food a growing part of NCC's academic mission. There are what might be called integrated activities, such as the farm's getting fifteen five-gallon buckets each week of compostable food waste from the school's dining service, and the on-campus farmers' market that's held in the main courtyard every Thursday. But there are also plans under way to build a year-round facility dedicated to food studies and food science, both of which will be degree-granting programs. The timetable calls for a grand opening in 2021. In the meantime, Kelly is infusing this robust community college with a fervor for food and farming that borders on the religious. To that end, his students are bound to carry the gospel of healthy eating and sustainability with them for the rest of their lives.

Farmland

Farming in the Lehigh Valley isn't limited to educational programs; the valley remains a vital food-producing region. It contains one thousand farms whose products find their way to consumers through farmers' markets, farm stands, community-supported agriculture (CSA) shares, farm-to-table restaurants, grocery stores, and farm-to-school programs. As of 2013, the Lehigh Valley's producers added $17 million to the local food economy. In spite of the contribution of agriculture, however, eight areas within the valley are experiencing limited access to fresh food.

As of 2018, 110,000 acres in Lehigh Valley—about 22 percent of the land mass—are devoted to agricultural use, down from 153,000 acres in 2007. The decline in acreage is propelled in large part by development in the Lehigh Valley. To offset that pressure, the Commonwealth of Pennsylvania and the counties of Lehigh and Northampton, both of which include portions of the city of Bethlehem, have combined to preserve about five hundred farms totaling fifty thousand acres, making these government-financed initiatives among the most aggressive farmland-preservation efforts in the country.

As in many regions where a high-density population bumps up against remaining farmland, Lehigh Valley farms struggle to remain economically viable. Generally speaking, smaller fruit and vegetable producers and specialty meat producers are doing better financially than, say, larger commodity producers such as dairies. If you're selling into local markets, retailing at a farmers' market, for instance, your margins will be better than a dairy farmer who is forced to sell into commodity markets. A good example of a long-standing farm operation that succeeds by directly serving the Lehigh Valley's consumers is Scholl Orchards.

As I'm waiting to talk to Ben Scholl, one of three siblings who run their family's farm, a van from the Northampton Meals on Wheels program pulls up to the combined apple shed, cider press, and farm office.

Ben, thirty-eight, whose broad shoulders and ruddy complexion leave little doubt as to his chosen career path, is using a forklift to load a pallet of apples into the van. Another pallet off to the side, I will later learn, is waiting for a truck from Second Harvest Food Bank. Sometimes this much generosity toward charities is an indication that sales aren't going so well. Not in this case. When the hyperenergetic Ben catches his breath and finally sits down for a chat, I tease him by asking if he had arranged the Meals on Wheels pickup for my benefit. He laughs it off and says, "No way! I sell to them at a discounted rate. They come every week without fail." Then I learn that five hundred gallons of their hard cider are going to Eight Oaks Craft Distillers to make applejack, and that another batch of cider is going to Sol Artisan Ales for its burgeoning hard cider market. ("This segment is exploding!" Ben told me.) Who said good deeds and alcohol don't mix?

Scholl Orchards was established in 1948 and is now managed by Ben; his sister, Martha; and his brother, Jake. (In a small-town coincidence, the farm stand where we're sitting abuts the Hoffman family's back property line, bringing me full circle to my conversation with Jake Hoffman.) The main site is in Bethlehem's city limits, but the Scholls own another eighty acres about forty minutes away, where they grow apples, peaches, and vegetables. As Ben put it, their size makes them "the largest of small farms." But it's big enough to support three families, even if the brothers get their health insurance through their wives' off-farm jobs and each works sixty hours, seven days a week.

The secret to their success is that 70 percent of their crop is sold retail. The biggest share goes to the nearby Easton Farmers' Market, followed closely by sales from their own farm stand. The remainder is sold wholesale to Lafayette College, restaurants, and their discount customers such as Meals on Wheels. Ben said, "Buy Fresh Buy Local has been the biggest driver for us. My business has grown like crazy in the last ten years—sales at the farmers' market and farm stand are up twenty-five percent—because people want to have a relationship with a farm." Buy Fresh Buy Local is an organization that promotes a variety of direct farmer-to-consumer sales venues, including farmers' market, CSAs, and Farm to School programs. They are also responsible for conducting regional food assessments that enable farmers, consumers, and policy makers to have a better understanding of the local food landscape.

Perhaps the biggest "aha!" moment came when I bit into an apple that Ben gave me—which was so good it practically brought tears to my eyes. What's astonishing is that it's mid-April, and this apple, a cross between a Honeycrisp and a Fuji, had been picked the previous September. I had not realized how the advances in food handling and storage technology have contributed to the viability of local farming. (Squeezing out the carbon from the apple right after harvest does wonders for preservation.) With improved apple varieties and storage techniques, Ben tells me they sell their own apples from September until June, when peach season begins. That allows the Scholls to sell fresh fruit year-round.

When I ask Ben about product pricing and how farmers' markets have developed a high-end, elitist image, he puffs up his chest and tells me that his prices are competitive with Walmart. "My guilt gets the better of me if I charge more than fifty cents for a zucchini." He's optimistic about his work, never giving off an iota of the "ain't it awful" vibe I unfortunately hear from many farmers. Ben believes that farming in the Lehigh Valley is economically healthy and viable, and he is quite certain that it will only get better.

Should I Stay or Should I Go?

As I found throughout my Bethlehem meanderings, the association between art and food is ubiquitous. One person who works at their intersection is Kate Armbruster, a staff person with the SouthSide Arts

District. She's a Bethlehem native who graduated from Lehigh University and stayed on because of her love for food and gardening. Kate's start in the food world took place when she was still a student at Lehigh, and her story is in many ways emblematic of the challenges that Bethlehem still faces.

Kate was hired by the university ostensibly to start a community garden on the campus, but she acknowledges that the real agenda was to improve town and gown relations, which had become a bit frayed over the years. For three years, she managed a quarter-acre garden that provided food to New Bethany Ministries. The project continues today at a reduced scale and without Kate's participation. Afterwards, she worked on garden projects that included fruit-tree plantings along the South Bethlehem Greenway, a lovely linear park that runs east-west through the town and roughly parallel to the river. She also helped establish a community garden at Third and New Streets that was later moved to the greenway. She loves the artistic flair that the Arts District brings to her work, including public planter beds made from Bethlehem Steel's old steel pipes and sculptured metal bike racks.

In spite of these developments, you hear in Kate's voice what you often hear from other young people in cities that are big enough to spark excitement, but not necessarily big enough to sustain it. After all, it's Bethlehem, not Brooklyn, and the question that always sits on the lips of those like Kate is, "Should I stay or should I go?" On the one hand, she says, "A new era is coming to south Bethlehem," and on the other, she's upset by the fact that the resources needed to foment a Lehigh Valley version of Brooklyn are limited. "There are no bikeways," she tells me. "I saw a bicyclist hit by a car who almost died!"

Similarly, food festivals abound, but their popularity creates unnecessary competition. A festival called Veg Fest, which was held on the greenway, became so popular that people would wait in hour-long lines to get a meal from their favorite veg truck. For no reason that she can discern, Veg Fest moved to the North Side. "The North Side doesn't need another festival. It's a shame!" As Jake Hoffman, another native millennial who did leave Bethlehem, said, "That bridge over the river connects people from the North Side and the South Side, but it's still a defining divide."

As one might hope, there is usually more harmony in the region's elementary schools, where gardens and healthy-eating initiatives are becoming as common as chalkboards. Thanks to the Kellyn Foundation (not a grant-making foundation but a highly branded nonprofit service provider), access to healthy, fresh food has expanded dramatically in the Lehigh Valley. *Kellyn,* a Celtic word meaning "warrior princess," seems an apt way to describe the foundation's cofounder, Meagan Grega, a physician and evangelist for healthy eating. "I want to make healthy food choices the easy choice," "Food is medicine," and "Coca-Cola is as bad for kids as smoking" are just some of the phrases that she and her work partner, Eric Ruth, use to react to what they describe as Bethlehem's "perfect storm." Changing lifestyles, less physical activity due to the end of factory and farm jobs, and the growth in processed and fast food have expanded waistlines and accelerated diabetes rates.

Kellyn's response has been multifaceted. A mobile market in the form of a twenty-seven-foot-long trailer goes to places such as Bethlehem's senior and low-income housing, bringing fresh food, much of it locally produced. The market handles Double Up Food Bucks for SNAP recipients and "veggie scrips," which are issued by St. Luke's Hospital to patients in need of additional healthy-eating incentives. As Meagan puts it, "We are the farmers' market in these low-access neighborhoods." Kellyn Kitchens are healthy-eating facilities in schools and community centers that provide training for families and individuals interested in improving their diets. Related to the kitchens is Kellyn Schools, which now have a presence in all sixteen of Bethlehem's elementary schools. In addition to a food instruction program for grades three through five, Kellyn Schools has initiated school gardens as part of its food teaching program.

Taking Care of Our Own

Just as I was falling into woodchuck holes at East Forty Acre Farm, I'm now catching the toe of my boot on slabs of sidewalk cracked and lifted by impertinent tree roots. Diane Elliott is giving me a walking tour of the South Side neighborhood that rings New Bethany Ministries, the multiservice, multi-care facility she directs. Diane wants me to see the gritty side of Bethlehem that is physically close to the arts and restaurants of the historic downtown but miles apart when it comes to income. "The Lehigh Valley has sixty-two thousand food-insecure people," she tells me. "New Bethany's food pantry gives out a three-day supply of food to three hundred households each month, and we serve one hundred seventy-five people a hot meal each day." There are twenty-one emergency food pantries scattered across Bethlehem, and right now we're walking through the part of the city where most of those food pantry recipients live.

This is also where former steelworkers raised their families. Once solidly middle-class, it got a bit tattered at the edges, declined, and eventually became the place where people who were struggling to get by could find cheap rents. But even that is changing, with homes that used to go for $20,000 now selling for $200,000 as more folks with means discover Bethlehem's attractions. This only pushes the renters into tighter and more difficult surroundings. "According to HUD data, a fair market rent for a two-bedroom apartment is almost eleven hundred a month," said Diane. "To say that we have a housing crisis here is an understatement." That is a good part of the reason she prides herself on New Bethany's commitment to providing shelter for the most

needy—thirteen transitional family units and fifteen single-room occu-
pancy (SRO) units.

As we're settling into a booth at a nearby coffee shop largely populated
by Lehigh students, I ask Diane, who is sixty-eight and an attorney, why
she continues to run a place that by her own admission is a 24-7 job.
The answer she gives is a very personal one. "I was treated badly as a law
student and as a lawyer. I was told by male lawyers that women can't be
good lawyers, because they cry. Every time I'd walk into the courthouse,
I had to show my credentials, even though the guards never asked the
male lawyers." As a result of this prejudicial treatment, she became a
public defender. But when the public defender's office found out she
was pregnant, they let her go. At that point, she'd had enough, which is
when she came to work for New Bethany.

After a long and effective tenure at New Bethany, Diane plans to
retire soon. That's not an admission that she's ready to walk away from
her larger mission of advocating for those who need housing, food, and
jobs. In spite of the C-Town grocery store, for instance, she thinks that
the South Side is still a food desert, so one of her crusades will be to find
a full-line supermarket to locate there. And she also plans on speaking
out when the occasion calls for it. This happened recently when a few
blustering politicians got on their high horses to repeat the old saw about
fraud among welfare recipients. When she wrote an op-ed that defended
recipients of public assistance, and then asked about the billions of dollars in fraudulent behavior on the part of bank executives, she received a
number of threatening emails. That's not likely to stop her.

It turns out that one of Diane's "partners in crime" is Olga Negron.
Between the two of them, they've been fighting the good fight in south
Bethlehem for a couple of decades. Olga serves on Diane's board of
directors; Diane helps Olga and other women and people of color get
elected to local office. They both share a story of resilience in the face of

adversity and a refusal to accept second best for the people they represent. The interaction between diversity and change remains Bethlehem's guiding narrative—a relatively small city with a powerful past searching for a new identity that encompasses the depth and breadth of its population.

Olga suggests that we get a cup of coffee at Café the Lodge, a restaurant and bakery that is run by and for people recovering from mental health illnesses. It's a little rough around the edges, the service has its challenges, but the scone I was served was pretty good. In a way, it's Olga's kind of place—give people a chance to make something of themselves while giving back to the community. "I grew up in a food environment," she tells me. "In Puerto Rico, we had two hundred chickens, three avocado trees, guava and mango trees; my father built and ran a local supermarket in the mountains. He could look at a live pig and tell you exactly how much meat was on it."

A Walmart moved into her area and killed off her father's store. Her work as a small farmer, cook, and store clerk disappeared, but she took up another avocation that she had managed to master along the way—dress and costume making. Moving to Austin, Texas, she found herself designing costumes for Hollywood filmmakers and then making them for such actors as Robin Williams and Drew Barrymore. While that was all very exciting for a young woman, her heart was still in social change, which led to a stint as a community organizer for the Head Start program. Organizing and helping those who were injured and used up by the warehouse industry were the natural antecedent to running for political office. All that community engagement is probably why she was the highest vote-getter in a recent election for the City of Bethlehem's eight city council seats. And just in case you think she forgot her food roots, she had three daughters along the way, all of whom are vegetarians today.

There is a personal stake that runs deep in Bethlehem. It manifests itself among people like Diane Elliott, Olga, and Kelly, who aren't going to be beat down by the "slings and arrows of outrageous fortune" or old ways, old boys, or the old guard. It includes people like Diane LaBelle, Rich, Kate, Javier, and Ben, whose roots in the community are strong and whose commitment is unwavering. Resilience in Bethlehem is more or less wired into its residents' genetic code, given the hits they've taken. I think of Jake Hoffman's dad, who switched from accountant to train engineer. As Diane Elliott said to me, "I know what it's like to be laid off. Everyone knows someone who has lost a job in Bethlehem."

While many efforts, small and gargantuan, are under way to reinvent Bethlehem, all voices are not necessarily being heard equally, nor is there the kind of coordination necessary to take the next big step. In the food world, the Lehigh Valley Food Policy Council is chipping away at the problem. Under the direction of Sue Dalandan, the council has been pushing local and state governments to do more to counter food insecurity and farmland loss. This includes getting more needy children enrolled in federal nutrition initiatives like the Summer Food Service Program (SFSP), which has traditionally been underutilized. There are also efforts to improve communication among the valley's numerous emergency food providers—a longtime challenge for these mostly private, volunteer-run groups.

Even Olga Negron, who is as close to local government as you can get, acknowledges that city hall is not doing enough to support food system initiatives. To date, the private sector has provided most of that kind of funding, including the Lehigh Valley United Way, which distributed about $350,000 to food projects in 2017. The Sands Casino has funded Buy Fresh Buy Local as well as other food ventures. St. Luke's Hospital has done the same. But even with these institutions stepping up, the philanthropic support is not enough, nor is it sufficiently coordinated to have the bigger impact necessary to provide all residents with equal access to healthy and affordable food. Who will fill that gap?

Because they are often the philosophical framers of life's dilemmas, I will give Bethlehem's artists the last word. In this case, it comes from two Bethlehemites who are active in Touchstone Theatre, an alternative-experimental performance group that's as cheeky as it is forthright. Bill George is the theater's co-founder and is currently coordinating an ambitious project called *Festival UnBound*, scheduled for a public debut in 2019. He is assisted by Christopher Shorr, a professor of theater at Moravian College. In essence, they are both pushing the boundaries of the community's consciousness by asking Bethlehem, "What is our identity, now that steel is no longer our identity?" Bill sets the stage with an existential brainteaser that goes something like this: "Now that our community is unbound by the steel industry, we are free to be something else. What do we do with our freedom? What do we become?"

Interestingly, both men have food stories that underscore this existential question. Bill's father was a farmer, he himself lives on a thirty-two-acre farm, and he brings a sense of mindfulness to food, art, and spirituality. Christopher was in the restaurant business, often uses food and its connection to culture to train young actors, and sees food as a way to bring a community together and to heal old wounds. "Theater and food are very similar because people come together to experience something, whether in seats looking at a stage or at a dining room table sharing food." Echoing Christopher, Bill said, "Theater is like food, we make a play from our lives, and we make meals from our food."

At the heart of these flights of artistic fancy lies a faith in people's judgment to choose the identity that's best for them and to distinguish between artifice and authenticity. Like Olga, who has cast her lot with individuals and the grass roots, not corporations, Bill and Christopher look askance at the "big arts organizations" and the big money that has

CHAPTER 2
Alexandria, Louisiana

My first daylight view of Alexandria, Louisiana, was from the Holiday Inn's seventh floor. A hot-pink sun was rising through the mist of the nearby Red River, which wrapped itself around the city's northeast border on its way to the Mississippi Delta. The river drains a vast, rural agricultural plain cultivated mostly for cotton, pecans, and soybeans. But like the city that the river lazily bypasses, its waters suspend molecules of a tough and sometimes brutal past as well as the sparks of a bright and hopeful future.

Bleary eyed from a late-night arrival, I take shuffling steps to the elevator for a ride to the breakfast buffet. The elevator's electronic signals tell me I'm on the eighth floor, even though I'm awake enough to know I'm on the seventh, which also happens to be the hotel's top floor. As I enter the lobby, I'm welcomed by the 8:00 a.m. chimes of the United Methodist Church across the street. However, my cell phone tells me it's really 8:11. The food arrayed against the restaurant's long wall ranges from heavy to heavier to heaviest, which accurately reflects the weight range of the fifty or so southern-accented patrons who dig into the morning fare with gusto. Though I'm sporting a few extra pounds myself, I feel positively anorexic in comparison to those around me.

Skipping the Special $9.95 Breakfast Buffet, I decide to chase down a tip I had received about a place called the Tamp & Grind, a cool little coffee shop that turned out to be only six blocks from the Holiday Inn. Unfortunately, at that hour, its hip vibe was shared only by me and the purple-haired barista, who did her best to fill the shop's yawning emptiness with her cheery mug. I had not expected Alexandria to deliver a smaller version of New Orleans's 24-7 get-down-and-boogie mood, but neither did I expect the heart of downtown to be enveloped in a funereal gloom. Gazing onto the silent streets through the café's floor-to-ceiling windows, I noted that it took nearly eight minutes for one form of human life to pass—a city transit bus with a single rider.

The scene at the Holiday Inn breakfast buffet is not an anomaly. If anything, it's a ground truthing for a pending southern tragedy. A report issued by the Robert Wood Johnson Foundation in 2016 found that Louisiana had the highest rate of adult obesity in the nation—36.2 percent in 2015, up from 22.6 percent in 2000. Related to those figures was a diabetes rate that is 12.7 percent of adults, fifth highest in the country, and a 39.3 percent hypertension rate, the fourth highest. Like much of the South, where obesity rates often run 50 percent higher than the "skinnier" regions of the Northeast and West Coast, Alexandria doesn't skimp on the fat and sugar. At a lunch meeting at Wildwood Pizza, a lovely Italian restaurant that buys lots of locally produced food, it was difficult to order a salad that wasn't loaded with bacon or pepperoni, or pizza that wasn't smothered in barbecue sauce. Ads running on my car radio were dominated by upcoming NASCAR races and the Monster Truck Exposition ("Good, clean family entertainment!"), none of which I can assume was sponsored by the Louisiana Vegetarian Society.

My early impressions of the state of the state's diet were confirmed at a meeting of the Louisiana Food Fellows leadership group. Food Fellows is a program of the Central Louisiana Economic Development Alliance (CLEDA), a nonprofit devoted to resurrecting Central Louisiana from the socioeconomic doldrums. These dozen or so fellows are early- to mid-career professionals and activists who come from farming, government agencies, and various nonprofit organizations. When the Fellows were asked what they saw as the most glaring weaknesses in the region's food system, most of them cited limited access to healthy and affordable food, food deserts, not enough farmers' markets, the lack of (and need for) more food education for younger people, little understanding of how to use fruits and vegetables, and people locked into old, unhealthy foodways.

But I was not in Alexandria simply to confirm my assumptions about the Deep South. Thanks to tips that led me to farmers' markets, great restaurants, brewpubs, and community gardens, I would learn that Alexandria's food scene was not a cholesterol-clogged heart on the brink of stroke. It was instead beating strong with an infusion of new blood, ideas, and leadership. After the Food Fellows' dismal appraisal of Central Louisiana's food system, they proudly asserted that the "upside" consists of an emerging network of new and young farmers, more school gardens, and, yes, more healthy food. The proverbial glass was clearly filling up, not emptying out. In fact, the Fellows' own engagement was a sign that their optimism was warranted. When that class of Food Fellows closed in late 2017, one woman chose to leave a good job to become a community garden activist while three others joined the Central Louisiana Food Policy Council as volunteer members.

John Cotton Dean

I pulled up a seat across the table from John Cotton Dean at the Tamp & Grind. His title, Director of Regional Innovation for CLEDA, seemed a size too big for his youthfulness, but his five years of organizing community development projects across ten Louisiana parishes had earned him every syllable. His lack of a southern accent forced me to ask about his middle name, but he's from Washington State by way of Iowa, and Cotton is coincidentally an old family name, not some affectation he adopted to ingratiate himself to the region's good ole boys.

He tells me that CLEDA is an alliance of the region's businesses, government, and social institutions—not unlike a chamber of commerce—that is using a multifaceted strategy to build the prosperity of ten parishes (counties) in Central Louisiana. Food and food system work, in all its dimensions, is a part of this strategy.

John's story of Alexandria is one of a rapid, from-the-bottom-up renaissance. "When I came here five years ago, there was only one coffee shop, now there are several." By "several" we are referring to independent cafés, not chains like Starbucks or Shipley Do-Nuts, and a number that fluctuates too often—mostly upward—to provide an accurate count but is far more than one. Brewpubs, a Friday evening Art Stroll, a farmers' market that has expanded to 15 vendors, and a host of food and farm initiatives are all products of a business-oriented community development strategy seasoned with a healthy dose of local entrepreneurism.

Looking out the windows onto the street, I see a vacant two-story building with the remnants of a sign that says RIVER CITY MARKET. John explains that this was a public market that fell on hard times but is now slated for redevelopment after it was taken over by a local businessman. Just across the street from that building is something called the Music Office Co-Op, which shares instruments and recording space for local musicians.

But what caught my eye just outside the Tamp & Grind were two homeless women—one black, one white—sharing the final drags of a cigarette while ensconced at the street's curb. They are wrapped in a rough kind of congeniality, laughing at some common joke, a salve perhaps for darker moments.

"One-third of Alexandria is black," John tells me, "but you wouldn't know that based on who shows up at our meetings." John's frustration is clear as he tells me of his attempts and those of others to bring white and black neighbors together. "There are so many groups trying to bridge the racial divide, but they are mostly talk and no action." Yet he still hopes that food might be the region's racial elixir.

John speaks and moves with a kind of gentle buoyancy that defies despair. His previous title was Director of Rural Prosperity, one that fits his upbeat personality to a tee. It also reflects CLEDA's aspirational development philosophy, one that builds on the community's existing resources and avoids the "ain't it awful" scarcity mentality. This attitude is immediately evident at CLEDA, which uses the quasi-celebrational term "makers" to describe those who produce something—almost any good or service—that can be sold and adds to the common wealth of the community.

At a CLEDA-sponsored Makers Morning event, small business entrepreneurs, farmers, artists, and craftspeople gather to lend one another support while receiving coaching from CLEDA staff. In a more traditional economic development vein, CLEDA also conducts business development and retention initiatives for everything from manufacturing facilities to new-tech start-ups. One regional effort, for instance, would develop a 1,600-acre former airpark as a site for new and expanding businesses. While more traditional businesses may dominate CLEDA's agenda, food and farming are now recognized as essential to Louisiana's revitalization. According to one CLEDA report ("Strategies for Growing Central Louisiana's Food Economy," 2015), the region's 1.4 million acres of farmland are producing half a billion dollars of agricultural value annually. While most of that goes into feed crops and processed foods, CLEDA claims that $91 million in value could be added to the local economy if local consumers each directed five dollars per week to local food purchases. To that end, John informs me that he was

CLEDA's first "food hire," followed shortly by Allison Tohme, Farmers' Market Program Developer, and Bahia Nightingale, Director of the Local Food Initiative. Together, this trio looks for every opportunity to leverage food and farming for the social and economic growth of Central Louisiana.

Art Stroll, Food Crawl, and Beer Brawl

What a difference a few hours can make! As the humid October darkness settled over downtown Alexandria, the previously somnambulant streets gradually filled with police barriers, hook-and-ladder trucks stringing lights and banners from streetlamps, and live music pulsing heavy and raw up and down the filling blocks. Vendors assembled their tables and tents stocked with everything from schlock to some items that might pass the art test, provided they were graded on a curve. No matter. Alexandria was alive with food, beer, and no small amount of human sweat.

I joined the festivities with a couple of pints at Finnegans Wake on Third Street, barely a block from the bridge over the Red River to Pineville. It was a spacious and authentically woody rendition of a Dublin establishment that might be frequented by Joyce, though one online reviewer said it was more Savannah-Irish than Irish-Irish. Whatever. The vibe was right, and the lean, tattooed bar mistress who explained the draft selections to me had a universality about her that would let her blend into Boulder, Brooklyn, or Boston. I chose a Great Raft Commotion Pale Ale from Shreveport, Louisiana. Great body, robust taste, and at five bucks for sixteen ounces, it was a good deal. Aside from the cigarette smoke from the outdoor tables at Finnegans (some southern habits die harder than others) wafting through the doorway occasionally, the pub was fun and filling.

Back on the "stroll," I momentarily bypass the vendors and merriment to walk along the river. My instinct for water proved serendipitous as I soon came upon the River Oaks Square Arts Center, a lovely museum whose mission is "to promote contemporary visual arts while providing educational programming that stimulates interest in, exhibition of, and appreciation for visual artists and their work." As part of Art Stroll, the center's doors were open, admission to the galleries was free, and the stylishly dressed crowd was enjoying the freely passed trays of wine. The food on the tables was pleasant, but it was the food on the walls that caught my eye. Every gallery was filled with soulful still lifes of persimmons, cherries, grazing sheep, and landscapes of overgrown pastures and broken fences. A pair of six-foot-long spoon and knife sculptures was suspended from another wall in case I felt the urge to "dig in."

Food as art was clearly on display that evening at River Oaks, but I later discovered that the art of food makes its presence known every May as one of the art center's biggest fund-raising events. Known as Men Who Cook & Men Who Mix, the event invites local food enthusiasts, chefs, and guys who are simply into food to prepare their favorite dish or drink recipes for taste testings. Apparently, the event draws a crowd of well over five hundred people each year and has been dubbed by those in the know as a "community favorite." Food as art and food as fund-raiser, and food as a way to get people out on the street, into the restaurants and pubs, and add a bit more communality to community life.

Returning to the stroll, I notice the crowds are respectable in size but not overwhelming. The music and lights in a small park vibrate but don't send my sixty-seven-year-old sensory organs into retreat. I stop at a vendor table stacked end-to-end with used vinyl records where a guy my age with a long gray ponytail sits. Pawing through some old rock 'n' roll LPs, I come upon a Bob Seger album not currently found in my collection. "How much?" I ask the dude. "Ten." It's a deal and we shake hands.

I'm hungry and need to eat, but consistent with my nonexistent restaurant-research methods, I have no idea where to go. So, I resort to the tried-and-true eatery-selection criteria I employ when I'm in a strange city—find a restaurant with an intriguing building façade and warm interior lighting; success is sure to follow! Clinging to Third Street and the stroll's undiminished hubbub, I pass several candidates to finally settle on a fine-looking art deco building that houses the Diamond Grill. Formerly the site of Schnack's Jewelers, the renovated interior retains the soft lighting, dark woods, and a dramatic staircase associated with the venerable downtown department stores of yore.

The menu has a strong local flair and advises me that the Diamond Grill participates in Fresh Central, a CLEDA-sponsored Central Louisiana–grown program. It urges me to "enjoy locally purchased foods!" I start with a gumbo that has the pungent scent of the morning bayou about it, but is so deliriously mellow that it melts slowly into the far reaches of my mouth. The spices were perfectly understated, which left me musing, *What was that I tasted?* I chose the Fish Louisiane for my entrée, a red snapper reeled in from somewhere in the Gulf. While it was grilled just right, the chef succumbed to the unfortunate southern tendency to smother excellent ingredients with a heavy cream sauce. My poor snapper was pleading for air. But the too-rough treatment of the fish was redeemed by a side of green beans whose "snap" had been so well preserved that one gave off an audible *pop* when I discreetly broke it in half.

As I paid the tab—an amount commensurate with the quality of the meal—I noticed that an Art Stroll parade was passing the Diamond Grill's front door. Indeed, the restaurant's website proclaims that "every parade or event starts or ends at our front door!" As I watched oversized stick figures in the shape of horses and dinosaurs festooned with strings of blue lights pass by, I wondered if there was another restaurant in America that could make such a claim, or more precisely, why it would even matter. But then I remembered I was in Louisiana, home of Mardi Gras, which also explained the remnants of beads I had seen scattered in Alexandria's shade trees.

Quality of Life

While the Friday night Art Stroll may appear to be a more or less spontaneous outburst of Louisiana joie de vivre, there's more to it than meets the eye. To the casual visitor, Alexandria's understated demeanor can sometimes feel as if somebody of minor importance has just died, making the Stroll's revelry appear to be not much more than an extravagant wake. But in fact, it was the recognition that Alexandria was in trouble that led to action by entrepreneurs, CLEDA, and the City of Alexandria. For the municipal government's part, they knew how to do festivals. Public safety officials and the local permitting offices were required to close streets, manage traffic flow, and ensure sanitary food. In other words, their job requires everyone to be in compliance with the myriad things that local government bureaucracies are responsible for but drive everyone else crazy. Most important, they knew this was the way to bring people downtown, a perennial challenge facing small cities that have lost their vigor due to structural changes in the region's economy and the dispersal of populations to the suburbs. Beyond making food a cause for merriment, city government plays a relatively small role in Alexandria's local food scene.

That fuzzy term "quality of life" comes to mind. It's a sense of fulfillment derived from a place and associated activities that we generally take for granted, except when it's not there. But when mayors and planners tell us that they are trying to promote it, the phrase sounds vague and its achievement dauntingly elusive. From CLEDA's perspective, Central Louisiana needs to be able to attract businesses. And according to some surveys, quality of life ranks as one of the top three or four factors that businesses consider when selecting a new site for relocation or expansion.

The cynical among us, this writer included, assumes that corporations seek out areas where taxes and wages are low. Depending on the industry and its need for natural resources (to either use or abuse), they also favor locations where environmental regulations are lax. But as the workforce grows more technologically sophisticated and better educated, companies are in a race to attract the best talent possible. For that growing pool of professionals, whose palates are as educated as their minds, quality of life does not include watery coffee, anemic beer, a night out at Denny's; and maybe most important, substandard schools. Alexandria's growing restaurant, farmers' market, café, brewpub, and art scenes will draw and retain young and mid-career professionals. Afford-able housing, safe neighborhoods, and functioning public schools may still be the most immediate criteria for people selecting a place to live. However, humanity's ascending hierarchy of needs increasingly includes the desire for a sense of community and enriching social, cultural, and even spiritual lives. In other words, there are growing signs that Amer-ican industry's race to the bottom is starting to turn in the other direc-tion, and that food and art are no small reason for that welcome reversal.

Taking Care of Our Own

From my description of Alexandria's food scene and its economic devel-opment strategies, one might rightfully think that the city cared only about a targeted elite. After all, Louisiana's overall poverty rate of 19.6 percent (2016) makes it's the second poorest state in the country, the same national ranking as its childhood poverty rate of 28.1 percent. In case someone is assuming that the city's emerging café and pub scenes insulate it from poverty, think again. Alexandria's poverty rate is 24 per-cent, making it a poor city in one of the nation's poorest states. And when poverty is so pervasive, food insecurity is not far behind—18.4 percent for Louisiana, which means that it also happens to have the nation's second worst hunger rate.

With numbers like those, Alexandria could add another one hun-dred farm-to-table restaurants to its streets and a thousand taps to its brewpubs and still not make much of a dent in these poverty measures.

Until economic development initiatives start to raise all ships, a large segment of the population must rely on a combination of public and private relief programs and services—such as the Food Bank of Central Louisiana.

I've walked into the lobbies of many food banks in my life, but never any quite like the one I saw at the Central Louisiana Food Bank. Instead of a single receptionist who directs you to the appropriate office, clients (yes, clients!) sit in a comfortable, well-lit waiting area before going to one of several intake windows, where they will receive help applying for SNAP benefits, a food donation from the food bank, or health insurance. Yes, people needing assistance in Central Louisiana can take advantage of the uniquely reasonable and utterly humane idea of "one-stop shopping." You, and sometimes your unhappy children, don't have to spend hours or even days driving or taking a bus to several locations to secure the help you need.

Jayne Wright-Velez started with the food bank as a Volunteers in Service to America (VISTA) worker in 1991. Today, she is the executive director and confesses without a murmur of repentance that "the food bank is a passion of mine, and it's been exciting to watch it grow." She ticks off its milestones such as going from virtually no staff to ten full-time and ten part-time staff, plus an astounding two thousand volunteers (a number that is a significant measure of both a community's desire to help their own as well as an innate commitment to food as a way to do it). She's especially proud of its "customer-focused client services center" which, along with its 109 member agencies (mostly food pantries), currently assists more than twenty-two thousand people per month. A large share of that assistance comes from the seven million pounds of food distributed each year, an amount that keeps pace with a steadily growing demand.

"We're good at counting the number of 'pounds in' and 'pounds out,'" Jayne notes ruefully, recognizing that more pounds of food won't stem the region's high poverty rate. But she also acknowledges that the food bank's dependency on food donations from the retail and whole-sale food industries ("We don't have the luxury of turning away *any* food donations," she tells me) won't slim down an obese and sick pop-ulation. This is why her earnest demeanor lightens considerably when she describes the food bank's forays into upping its produce game. The effort began with doubling its refrigeration capacity to hold more fresh fruits and vegetables. But the flagship of its healthy food initiative is the Good Food Project, a venture that includes seventy-four community gardens spread across its entire eleven parishes and serves over seventeen thousand people annually.

Designed to "reconnect people to the food they eat" the project places as much emphasis on education, especially for children, as it does on food production. That's why thirty of the seventy-four gardens—an astounding total number of gardens for a food bank to be overseeing—are planted on school grounds. As Jayne sees it, "we're not going to break the cycle of dependence" until the next generation learns how to eat healthy food. That's a process that begins with "hands in the dirt" and a wheelbarrow full of nutrition education. Jayne told me that the kids coming into the program simply don't know what vegetables are. Volunteers have to resort to flash cards with vegetable images on them to give children some basic knowledge.

All in all, the food bank sees the Good Food Project as a bridge between local food and the region's underlying food insecurity. A brief tour of the food bank's model garden with the project director, Frances Boudreaux, offers a glimpse into that connection. Immediately adjacent to the food bank's main warehouse, one-third of an acre of land is filled with multiple garden beds as well as kiosks and platforms where teaching and even therapeutic activities take place. Frances, an exceptionally spry woman in her sixties, explains how the multihued beds—collectively presenting themselves in the shape of a flower when viewed from one of the elevated platforms—serve as a kind of horticultural focal point for the larger community. "It's an intergenerational gathering place where we learn and grow healthier together," she tells me. While the overall effectiveness of the program is still largely anecdotal, its reach is substantial. And integrating gardening with food education with emergency food services—including access to programs like SNAP—illustrates the importance of linking up food initiatives.

Coordinating Community

So how linked up are Central Louisiana's many and varied food efforts? Are organizations coordinated? Do they avoid duplication and agree on the region's biggest needs? CLEDA sees the region through an economic development lens, but it is one that is both wide and discerning enough to embrace the value of most food enterprises, regardless of their commercial potential. On the other hand, at least according to some people I interviewed, the Central Louisiana Food Bank keeps to its mission and simply doesn't "get" economic development as a means to tackle poverty and hunger. The result of that viewpoint is that the food bank has so far refrained from joining the Central Louisiana Food Policy Council, which has the potential to create a more comprehensive food agenda for the region.

Attempts to improve collaboration in the region's food system are nascent. One showing promise is another CLEDA invention called Foodapalooza. This is a two-day event, started in 2012, that brings together people working in public health, public policy, economic development, and local food to identify common issues and to celebrate the region's local food movement. The 2018 Foodapalooza conference title was "Healthy People, Healthy Economies & Vibrant Places." Attendees heard from national experts such as former USDA official and nutrition expert Angie Tagtow. While not necessarily producing a regional food movement agenda—a road map of sorts that the participants can sign on to—Foodapalooza does turn the spotlight on food's economic and health benefits while providing networking opportunities for those engaged in the work.

One happy by-product is that Foodapalooza has captured the attention of the area's foundations. While fund-raising is always a challenge, Alexandria and its nearby environs are fortunate to have an emerging group of "food funders." In particular, Keller Enterprises, a family company with a historical business connection to Murphy Oil Soap, goes beyond just funding charitable food work. Keller has agricultural roots in the region that include the Inglewood Farm, a substantial operating farm that dates back to 1836. It produces commodity-scale cotton and soybeans but is rapidly transitioning to sustainable vegetable and meat production.

The farm also offers CSA shares, produce that goes to seven farmers' markets, online ordering, and numerous educational programs. According to one source, Inglewood's Saturday farmers' market "looks like a big-city farmers' market." Not only does Inglewood's high profile make a substantial contribution to Alexandria's food identity, but Keller Enterprises does as well, including a $1.1 million start-up grant to the Central Louisiana Food Bank's Good Food Project. Significant funding is also provided to CLEDA's Fresh Central food initiative. This kind of one-two punch from a single entity—a demonstrated commitment to sustainable production combined with community funding—is a big reason that Alexandria's food scene punches above its weight.

Similarly, the Rapides Foundation, founded in 1994, focuses its giving on health issues, including those related to diet. Interestingly, it also addresses economic development, viewing the region's standard of living and quality of life as determinants of individual health. CLEDA is just one recipient of Rapides's funding. The combination of Keller and Rapides doesn't mean that Alexandria's food system has all the funding it needs, but it does give an under-resourced small city and rural area some definite advantages.

Health and community development also come together through local and state food policy. This is why the Central Louisiana Food Policy Council has become an important player. So far, the council has focused on local food sourcing for the city, conducting outreach for the federal Summer Food Service Program (SFSP), and advocating for workplace health incentives. Concerning the latter point, the council worked directly with the State of Louisiana Department of Health's Well-Ahead Louisiana program to integrate locally grown, raised, and caught food into its work site cafeterias. In this way, it can encourage healthier food choices as well as offering an expanded market for Louisiana's producers.

Sometimes the council's work may not seem like much more than a series of minor actions that have little impact. But when the governing bodies of small towns like Jonesville (pop. 2,500), Boyce, and Colfax pass resolutions recognizing World Food Day or remove regulations that restrict the sale of local produce, as they did at the council's behest, public awareness of the value of a local food economy grows. Additionally, it draws attention to healthy eating, which is one of the council's goals for 2018. With the aid of three of CLEDA's Food Fellows, the council is developing a "tool kit" to help municipalities and private workplaces get healthier local food into their vending machines and cafeterias.

Bridging the Racial Divide

Events like Foodapalooza, food banks like Central Louisiana, and coalitions like the Food Policy Council make food a part of the community conversation. So far, however, they have not bridged the region's underlying divide: race. To better understand the area's long history of racism, John Dean suggested I travel to Colfax, a sleepy little town of 1,600 people only twenty-eight miles from Alexandria. By the side of what turns out to be one of only two main roads in town, I found five farmers and their pickup trucks selling their goods at the farmers' market. Nothing too remarkable here as far as Saturday morning markets go—a small number of customers were inspecting the fall fare of collards, squashes, jams and jellies; people were chatting good-naturedly over bushel baskets and truck beds. Two old guys in overalls were talking trash with each other. "I'm gonna put a sign on the back of your truck," one of them said to the other, "'Beware! Old Fart Driving.'" As Kate Littlepage, a local farmer and vocational agriculture instructor told me, "this market is less about food and more about community."

Somewhat more noticeable, at least for this Yankee, was that two of the five farmers were African American. My racial radar seems like it's always on these days, but the deeper I plunge into the South, the more blips I see on my screen. It turns out that I was picking up historical signals from the very soil where I was treading. Though the Colfax farmers' market was micro in size, its racial composition made it outsized in symbolism. Just over 145 years ago—Easter Sunday, 1873—upwards of 150 black people were massacred by a resurgent force of neo-Confederate white supremacists that went by the name of the White League, the predecessor to the Ku Klux Klan. Lacking social media and phone cameras, most of America didn't become aware of the massacre until hand-drawn illustrations appeared in *Harper's Magazine* one month later.

In 1950, the year I was born, an unrepentant Louisiana contingent with a dubious historical mission erected a marker in the vicinity of this clash. It read, COLFAX RIOT—ON THIS SITE OCCURRED THE COLFAX RIOT IN WHICH THREE WHITE MEN AND 150 NEGROES WERE SLAIN. THIS EVENT ON APRIL 13, 1873 MARKED THE END OF CARPETBAG MISRULE IN THE SOUTH. It took over fifty years for a more repentant contingent to remove the marker, but it stood all that time as a potent example of the same lies and deceptive messages that are resurgent today.

Calling it a "riot" instead of a massacre put the blame on a duly constituted and largely black state militia that was attempting to enforce the new enfranchisement of black residents. When most of those militiamen surrendered to the heavily armed white paramilitary force, they were gunned down in cold blood. To say that the number of slain "negroes" was 150 is probably an understatement since many of the bodies were thrown into the nearby Red River, never to be found or identified. Swept up in the river's current, many no doubt were carried past Alexandria.

Even in a hostile post-Confederate Louisiana, however, federal prosecutors managed to obtain convictions against three of the white attackers. But they would be thrown out by the Supreme Court (*United States v. Cruikshank*) in 1876 on grounds that enforcement of the Fourteenth and Fifteenth Amendments—protection of civil and voting rights—rested with the states, not the federal government. This ruling was effectively the final curtain call for the Reconstruction Era, ushering onto the stage one hundred years of Jim Crow.

If justice still is only a dim light on a far horizon, what do we do in the meantime? Standing by the side of the road with those five farmers, I was reminded of the events that led up to the opening of this market. When John started his job with CLEDA, he began organizing community economic development projects. He had reached out to the Colfax community in hopes of discovering low-cost ways of stimulating the local economy. On one of his first attempts, as he tells it, eight people gathered at a church one night in 2013 to discuss what could be done. Four of them were black and four were white, and each racial group sat separately on opposite sides of the room. Trust was low and the conversation was muted, moving along in fits and starts. After an hour of little or no progress, John suggested they take a break.

At the time, John was new to organizing work in racially divided communities like Colfax. Worried that the whole evening might be a bust, he was pleasantly surprised when all the people returned to the room. When he asked the group, what was one thing they wanted that they didn't have, they unanimously replied healthy food. When he followed up by asking what could be done to get healthy food, everyone landed on the idea of a farmers' market. The rest of the evening was devoted to working out the details of what was to become the place where I was then standing. John was as shocked as he was relieved when the meeting ended with everyone hugging one another.

Food is remarkable for its ability to heal the body and bring people together. Yet institutional racism in America, whose roots run deep and are watered regularly by white hatred, won't be undone by healthy, local food alone. At the same time, I don't see a viable pathway to closing the racial divide without a table where black and white can break bread side by side. As John said, "food was something they could do together." The farmers' market was only a beginning, and perhaps the more monuments to racism we can tear down, the more room we'll have for good local food.

A Long Row to Hoe

In Alexandria, I tasted and sipped some of Central Louisiana's best treats, and honed my aesthetic on southern art. I learned about public policy that is making eating healthy easier and private efforts to ensure that everyone has a seat at the table. This is the stuff that communities are made of, and food is the stuff that can raise a community's quality of life. But there is an image that stuck with me that I can't let go of.

As I was leaving Colfax on my way back to Alexandria, I detoured off the state road where the breakdown lanes were covered with windblown drifts of just-harvested cotton. I was headed to Boyce, one of the small places whose town council passed a resolution proclaiming World Food Day. I had received a tip that Boyce had built an open-air farmers' market structure, inspired no doubt by the oft-quoted movie line, "If you build it, and [they] will come." If it was there, I never found it, and if it was built, no one came, because there's no Boyce farmers' market among the eight listed for the region on Fresh Central's website. But what I did find in this town nestled on the shores of the Red River was rural poverty so extreme it made my bones ache.

Short side streets ran off one commercial corridor with virtually no commerce. I counted one gas station, several vacant stores, and one take-out fried chicken place. Run-down and abandoned homes alternating with vacant lots and makeshift auto shops dotted half a dozen side streets. The only buildings in worse condition were city hall and the police station—no property of much value, no property taxes, no public services. The churches, which almost outnumbered the town's other structures, were in reasonably good condition, perhaps echoing a collective hope that God would bring salvation to Boyce if its church folk kept their houses of worship in good repair. But like the visuals, the numbers tell the tale—out of Boyce's estimated population of one thousand, 41 percent of all residents and 52 percent of children live in poverty. And 75 percent are African American.

Perhaps the only thing that overwhelmed Boyce's stark poverty was the silence. It was Saturday afternoon, but there were very few cars on the road and no more than a few people were walking around. On the small porch of a wooden home that was in such disrepair it would be condemned in most developing countries sat an African American woman so morbidly obese that she couldn't move. The temperature was in the 80s and the sun beat down directly on her. I pulled over, got out of my car, and said hello. Smiling my best smile, I tried to engage her in conversation but to no avail. She barely acknowledged my presence. Wishing her a good day, I drove out of town feeling like my visit to Boyce was a tour of a social crime scene.

Will food save a town like Boyce, where the poverty rate is 70 percent higher than Alexandria's, which is 25 percent higher than Louisiana's, which is the second poorest state in the country? Will economic development in the style promoted by CLEDA ever bring Alexandria's poverty figures in line one day with those of Louisiana, and better yet, the United States? Jim Clinton, CLEDA's CEO, explains a three-pronged economic development strategy to me that sounds promising. It begins with promoting manufacturing, particularly existing manufactures, which doesn't mean trying to entice Mercedes-Benz into opening a new car factory in the region. These are companies not on any Forbes 500 list, but they are providing a reasonable number of decent-paying jobs. Second, there needs be a major emphasis on developing "knowledge platforms," economic development jargon for schools and skill-training programs. In Alexandria's case, the community college is locating down-town, which brings life to the city but also means more job-oriented education.

The third leg of development is regional innovation, and this is where food comes in, both directly and indirectly. "Innovation" in this context means channeled human creativity. Yes, you can be artistic, visionary, and capable of inventing a better mousetrap, but you and your busi-ness must make money and, hopefully, create jobs. So, I ask Jim, why food? "We commissioned a study," he tells me, "that [revealed] we were 'importing' $31 million more food than we produced. We had a 'trade deficit' that we could reduce by growing and selling more of our own, especially fruits and vegetables, and create businesses and jobs along the way." The import-export relationship also includes the region's larger commodity-scale agriculture that is exported, thus earning the region cash, which finds its way back into the local economy. Either way, value is added—the region produces more food for local consumption, thus displacing imports, and so-called export agriculture generates cash.

As evidence of work that's filling that gap, Jim cites a new lavender farm that's processing and selling oils and creams, a seasoning mix com-pany, a salad dressing company, and of course, brewing and brewpubs. Agritourism is on the rise as are farmers' markets and farm-to-table restaurants. While he notes that farmers' markets are not innovative per se anymore, if you don't have one in your community, which is the case for many Central Louisiana communities, then they are innovative.

At this point, Jim grows increasingly animated, which contrasts with an otherwise button-down demeanor that bespeaks a varied life in public administration. Among his previous assignments, he managed the transition of the New Orleans Superdome from a money-losing, corruption-ridden public enterprise into one that became profitable and privately run. He gets up from behind his large desk covered with reports and studies to pull down from a bookshelf an original issue of *The Whole Earth Catalog.* "It's still my bible that I consult regularly!" he tells me. Echoing a kind of MBA version of "small is beautiful," he dismisses the much-tarnished Earl Butz mantra "get big or get out" by saying, "That's not our model; we want people to be able to make it on a ten-acre farm."

This is where the indirect contribution of food as a part of regional innovation comes in. Jim explains that, "Food is a big part of your quality of life, and buying local is evidence of how good your quality of life is. By that, I mean the whole atmosphere, the whole feel of a place, a pride in what we grow. I see this at a farmers' market which builds community engagement and gives citizens a place to talk to other citizens. I don't see that happening at Kroger, whose idea of 'local' is something grown within a thousand-mile radius."

When food is placed within the larger, more robust model of economic development that Jim describes, its contribution starts to makes sense even though one can see that an economic revival may not be driven by food. Without the food component, however, community life will be devoid of much of what makes living in a community rewarding. But what about Boyce, and what about that poor, unhealthy woman sitting motionless on a humid day in the hot sun? Yes, there's the food bank, there are food stamps, and there is a dream that Boyce will one day have a farmers' market, but how will the growing food scene in nearby Alexandria help her?

I catch up with John Dean a few months after my visit, and I pose the dilemma to him of the woman on the porch. He reminds me that progress is incremental, that you have to commit to a long-term horizon, and you have to do that by continually developing the capacity of your organization and staff to work for that change. He cites signs of progress in just the last six months: the growing number of new farmers, including one who is growing and processing mushroom jerky. He tells me about a new professor in the Department of Allied Health at nearby Louisiana College who's reinvigorating the campus farmers' market and working with college dining on a new contract with Sodexo that will require more local food. He makes a point shared by many in the food movement that local food is not a fad anymore nor is it elitist. He's right, more robust food and farm economies are here to stay, and they are almost "normal." And with the guidance and determination of an organization like CLEDA and numerous partner organizations orbiting the same vision, a healthy economy and healthy food for all may one day become a reality. But will those benefits ever reach Boyce? Time will tell.

CHAPTER 3
Boise, Idaho

To say that Idaho is a "red state" is an understatement. I think the TV networks called the state's presidential vote for Donald Trump before the polls even opened on November 8, 2016. After all, Idaho Democrats hold a none-too-robust 17 percent of the state legislature's seats. Boise City Councilwoman Lauren McLean (Democrat) told me that when the city council voted to ban plastic bags, the state legislature preempted municipal authority to make such environmental laws. The state legislature was more interested in upholding Idaho's number two ranking as the nation's most "business friendly" state and possibly surpassing top-ranked Utah.

There are many other Idaho traits that don't easily recommend the state to progressive-minded people. For instance, it is one of the few states that still has a highly regressive food tax in spite of recent efforts by social justice advocates to eliminate it. The City of Greenleaf, less than an hour from Boise, garnered international attention in 2006, when its town council passed an ordinance "asking" all residents to *keep* firearms in the event that they might be overrun by refugees from Hurricane Katrina. Idaho is also home to the fast-food frozen French fry king, J. R.

Simplot, and factory dairy farms that use up cows and natural resources to churn out vast globules of processed cheese product.

So why was a left-leaning foodie like me interested in a place like this? In 2016 I had been invited to speak to the Summit on Idaho Hunger & Food Security and to conduct a training for the state's local food councils and coalitions. About a year later, I would give a similar food policy council training for the mayors and staff of six small Idaho cities. During these visits, I got in front of a combined three hundred food, farm, and health activists, and much to my surprise, I came away with the strong impression that, in spite of Idaho's rock-solid conservative credentials, the local food and food security movements are carving out some meaningful space for themselves.

Food certainly has its political moments, and links between environmental issues and food can incite political reactions. But even conservatives eat, and a political climate hostile to progressive actions doesn't necessarily suppress a vital food scene from emerging. My encounters with food activists, accompanied by local food tours, tastings, and interviews with fifteen Boise food-scene makers, piqued my interest in this funny if sometimes contradictory place. By the time I was ready to tap out some prose, I was convinced that you shouldn't judge a state by its voters, or its more extreme stereotypes, and that if you let your guard down, you just might discover unique pockets of splendor.

Local Food

There is no gauge that accurately measures the change in a place's food scene over the years. Yet a growing number of farm-to-table restaurants, gardening sites and programs, or even labels in an Albertsons supermarket aisle that reference ORGANIC, LOCAL, or GMO-FREE certainly suggest a strong shift in consumer preference. Old-timers may wax nostalgic for the diners that served them meat loaf and mashed potatoes, washed down with plastic cups of Budweiser or Coors. While they turn their florid noses up at today's brewpub chalkboards packed with exotically named suds, we sense that one group's grumbling is another group's contented sighs. But I haven't found a more reliable measure of change than that of the local food chronicler who, by being native to the place, possesses the historical perspective to write with accuracy and empathy.

That's why I was fortunate to come across Guy Hand, a native Idahoan who's the editor of *Edible Idaho*, a publication that provides a tantalizing survey of all-things-foodie across the state. Though his demeanor was modest and understated, his choice of a restaurant for our interview felt uncannily hip. It was an eatery and watering hole tucked inside the Modern Hotel and Bar (simply known as "the Modern" by locals), a nondescript 1960s-era motel. Thinking I'd made a mistake, I ducked inside to get directions only to discover that I was in the right place. After hanging out in the restaurant for a couple of hours, I would later concur with the following *Vogue* magazine review: "The Modern, a seedy motel-turned-stylish boutique hotel, has one of the buzziest bar scenes in town." And after sampling the food and drink list, I could see why it was so popular!

Hand probably picked the Modern for our meet-up to underscore his primary point about Boise—things sure have changed. "I grew up in Idaho but left in the 1970s," he told me. "I returned several years ago from Santa Barbara, and was shocked by how passionate people were, especially farmers, about food." As *Edible Idaho*'s photo editor, he became acutely aware of how much was going on—so much so, in fact, he "can't keep up with the number of food stories, even in the rural communities where a lot is also happening." Part of what excites him is the sheer quirkiness of the foodies he meets around the state who collectively keep his quarterly issues stocked with great material. "I came across an orchard in a remote canyon that was only accessible by water. The apples had a nearly transparent skin, and the flesh was a beautiful ivory color. I had never seen anything like them, and they were delicious!"

What seems to be universally recognized these days is that the food movement is far more grassroots and individualistic than other movements. This may account for some of its quirkiness, or it may simply be that food as an issue attracts those who are naturally quirky. (One local food advocate told me that Idahoans' natural disdain for government regulation spawned a great deal of small and creative food businesses, which encounter less red tape in Idaho than they do in other states). Hand contrasts the food movement's methodology with that of the environmental movement, which he describes as being largely directed by lawyers, not the hundreds of helter-skelter food activists and entrepreneurs on display in Boise, and as I was learning from Hand, throughout the state. As I explored the city's food terrain, what I saw time and again were people and small groups making their own individual statements while always keeping their ears to the ground for new opportunities, both for profit and nonprofit. As Hand notes, the statements can be as simple as your own garden or as complex as a city's comprehensive plan resplendent with worthy visionary ambitions. But at the same time that we may each be pursuing our own interests, food is bringing people together. Hand singled out people I would later meet like Janie Burns, Elaine Clegg, and David Crick as leaders of the region's food charge. But it's the eager consumers swarming the city's farmers' market every Saturday, or the dozens coming to public hearings at the state capitol advocating for an end to Idaho's food tax who are, as Hand put it, evidence that "food brings people together."

While Hand's enthusiasm for Idaho's food scene is palpable, it belies some of the state's darker moments that he's been forced to confront as a journalist. Taking photos of people waiting in long lines outside area food banks was distressing for him. He's grown increasingly concerned as well—to the point where I literally felt his sadness—that young farmers, local food's hope for salvation, are burning out at a rate that could ultimately undermine the movement. Though an outsider may be pleasantly amazed by the vibrancy of Boise's restaurant life, Hand sees it as still struggling. "After all, this is still a chain restaurant kind of town," he tells me, expressing worry that the city's creative cuisine class still gets too far out ahead of its customers. One example, which might be called the Valentine's Day massacre, took place when one notable restaurant served up a romantic menu item on February 14 that it called Duck Hearts on Fire! According to Hand, it barely received one quack.

But holding aside the occasional missteps, conflicts still plague Boise's food movement, as they do everywhere. Some years ago, the farmers' market, at the time only one, divided into two because one faction was more devoted to stricter definitions of "local" than another faction. In Hand's opinion, the resulting competition between them works to their mutual detriment. Even more distressing, however, are the eight-hundred-pound gorillas that roam Idaho's countryside. "When I leave the Boise oasis to visit the state's rural areas," Hand recounts, "I'm struck by the poverty." As in other places where land is cheap, regulations lax, and good-paying jobs hard to come by, the ugly side of America's food system finds an easy home in Idaho.

This is certainly the case with the state's confined agriculture feeding operations, known as CAFOs, or in less sympathetic circles, factory farms. Having covered the state's dairy industry for *Edible Idaho*, Hand characterizes the problems associated by CAFOs as "terrifying and shocking." Small dairy farmers have been driven out of business by big dairies. County commissioners who resisted making local permitting changes favorable to big dairy received threatening phone calls late at night. Exploitation of labor, much of it directed at undocumented immigrants, and environmental degradation that has polluted water previously used by the state's highly touted trout industry are some of the legacies of Idaho's big dairies. Having learned his lessons the hard way, that you can only drive into a brick wall so many times before you eventually die, Hand acknowledges these are state realities that you can't change, at least for now.

Boise is not Idaho. If the word "oasis" suggests a striking contrast between a small place and its vast surroundings—a place that offers considerable refreshment and relief from an otherwise inhospitable environment—then Boise is certainly the place where desert wanderers will want to tie up their camels. It has excellent farm-to-table restaurants— check out Red Feather Lounge and Bittercreek Alehouse. *Edible Idaho* is chock-full of stories and ads depicting a smorgasbord of local delights from the Boise Co-op to Idaho's vodka. (Potatoes aren't just for French fries.) The Idaho Farmers' Market Association coordinates forty-eight farmers' markets around the state, including a Boise mobile farmers' market that makes eleven stops each week at sites serving senior citizens. The two bustling Boise farmers' markets are so popular they virtually shut down the city every Saturday morning at the season's peak.

The city's enthusiasm for local food even extends into the schools. Boise High School offers a progressive environmental curriculum that includes a well-tended student farm a few blocks from its main campus. The school also hosts a local food-security summit every two years. On the day that I visited, teacher Ali Ward was directing about thirty shovel-bearing students preparing the soil for a winter cover crop planting. (When not instructing young people, Ali plays musical saw and washboard in a local band.)

And just in case you were worried that the state's large Mormon community (24 percent of Idaho) might dampen Boise's enthusiasm for alcohol, dozens of local microbrews, wineries, and several new hard cider labels, fueled by thousands of acres of nearby hops, vineyards, and orchards, will tempt the soberest citizen.

Even the briefest of Idaho's food scene tours would be incomplete without a tip of the hat to a longtime food activist and farmer, Janie Burns. Starting in 1989 on her Canyon County farm with seven chickens and first-day-ever farmers' market sales of twenty-seven dollars, Janie has been growing food and raising animals while developing projects and raising a little Cain. She and her sidekick, local educator Susan Medlin, cofounded the Treasure Valley Food Coalition which has launched a number of initiatives, including the Tomato Independence Project. This was a three-year community venture whose galvanizing slogan "End the tyranny of the tasteless tomato!" ignited a firestorm of enthusiasm for local food.

The project encouraged people to plant tomatoes everywhere—in public as well as private spaces—take tomato-growing classes, save seeds, make sauce, celebrate "Tomato Tuesday," read the book *Tomatoland*, and learn about the injustices that farmworkers face. Thousands of people got on board, especially when they hosted a "Bloody Mary" event that combined local tomato juice with, you guessed it, Idaho vodka! "The whole tomato project was the coalition's way of showing people they don't have to feel helpless when it comes to their food," Susan told me.

The coalition has also run a series of forums on the loss of the Treasure Valley's farmland, clearly an issue where red-state sensibilities clash with blue-state sensitivities. The roughly thirty-by-one-hundred-mile valley's beautiful, irrigated farms and deep bottomland soils are under siege from developers and an expanding home-buyer appetite for still moderately priced housing, a pleasant climate, and an endless horizon. Janie, who's possessed of an elegant syntax, refers to all of this as "lovely sprawl" that's filling Boise's fringe with "upper-crusty, McMansion-y" homes. Recognizing the current limits of Idaho food activism, she said, "There is a surge of interest in local food and food security, both from the public and the marketplace, [but] we all learned long ago to keep our heads off the skyline and avoid poking the bear." The "bear," in this case, is a rough network of industrial agriculture operators, pro-development forces, and archconservative ideologues.

The region's abundant farmland is not the only source of food production. Community gardens and urban farms abound in Boise, and also speak to the city's surprising diversity. One example is Global Gardens, a nonprofit farm training and refugee resettlement program whose vision is for "a community of culturally diverse individuals empowered to cultivate food, engage with the community, and become entrepreneurs." Anywhere from eight to fifteen refugee families participate in farmer-training activities, much of which takes place on half-acre lots allocated to each family. The lots are donated by local landowners, and refugees may stay there for up to three years. They also receive marketing assistance, which includes the opportunity to hone their skills and earn income by selling at Boise's two farmers' markets and the Boise Co-Op. For those refugees not inclined toward commercial-scale production, Global Gardens offers nine community garden sites in and around Boise. This gives them a chance to increase their self-reliance, especially by growing food traditional to their cultures and countries that can't easily be found in local retail outlets. A web of support from numerous nonprofits, private landowners, farmers' markets and the Boise Coop, and the City of Boise gives Global Gardens the resources it needs, but perhaps more important, upholds the value of community diversity.

Food is also a central theme with one prominent Boise training program that serves young adults ages sixteen to twenty years old who "face significant barriers to success." Bearing the appropriate name of Life's Kitchen, the program provides sixteen weeks of food-service and life-skills training for its participants. Participants get immediate job training by working in the program's café, catering, and contract food services, the latter of which provides meals for three Boise private schools.

The City Steps Up

I sat down with Boise City Council President Elaine Clegg to learn more about the city government's role in local food and farming. "Sat down," that is, only after Clegg, who is a very tall, slender woman in her sixties, rolled her bike out of the city hall elevator and set it beneath a sign taped to a waiting room wall that read, STAFF PARKING. Since the space was large enough to accommodate only one bike, I assumed this was a perk accorded only to the greenest of city officials.

Bicycling to and from work, however, was not the only way Clegg reinforced her environmentalist cred. First becoming interested in civic affairs through a Boise neighborhood association, she literally got her feet wet with regional land use policy when she fought to protect nearby wetlands from development in 1985. In a state that smiles favorably on all forms of development, Clegg had to find a way to stand up for the environment without being tarred as anti-growth. "I'm not antidevelopment," she told me, "I'm pro smart growth, and I'm pro farmland." You don't successfully navigate your way over Idaho's dangerous political terrain, even in a relatively progressive oasis like Boise, by taking extreme positions or using a strident tone. "I'm a 'middle broker,'" she adds. Yet she makes it clear that she values open space and the Treasure Valley's beautiful natural landscape, and healthy, local food. The way you realize those values is by laying the groundwork for change and looking for opportunities. In so doing, you maintain your credibility at all cost while recognizing that persistence is necessary.

Fortunately, there's much to build on in and near Boise if food and the environment are your passions. At the dawn of the twentieth century, Boise was defined by dams, water diversions, and what was and continues to be called the New York Canal. (See Wallace Stegner's *Angle of Repose* for an eloquent rendering of this period.) Much of the early irrigation engineering began crudely in the mid-1800s and was later boosted by the need for food production to feed the area's burgeoning mining camps—the promise of gold drawing men like no other temptation. But a chaos of competing water claims and the need for upstream water storage required the federal government to intervene. With congressional passage of the Reclamation Act of 1902—perhaps the region's first major piece of farm policy—the stage was set for Boise; Ada County, which contains the city; and nearby Canyon County to become agricultural powerhouses. This is the kind of engineering and public policy—seemingly arcane by today's standards—that made the region what it is today.

Cast your eyes just a bit beyond Boise's modest skyline, and your attention is immediately seized by the rolling foothills that, if the light and shadows are right, undulate across the horizon like massive coils of intestines. With foresight uncommon almost anywhere, Boise has acquired forty-three thousand acres of these hills and created 190 miles of trails. This smart growth intervention has so far prevented Boise from looking like areas of Southern California, where cookie-cutter subdivisions run rampant up and down barren flats and hills placing homes directly in the path of wildfires and mudslides.

City Councilwoman Clegg recognizes that protecting open space doesn't necessarily protect surrounding farmland, which has been under siege since the end of the Great Recession and the resurgence of the region's housing boom. Lacking robust farmland-protection policies such as the purchase or transfer of development rights (particularly the funding to support such policies), Boise's popularity as the West's newest destination city may place the region's food security at risk. Noting these challenges, Clegg and the city council are pursuing measures that are feasible within their jurisdictional boundaries that don't offend pro-growth opponents or undercut "Boise's reputation as a welcoming place," as Clegg put it. Urban agriculture, for instance, got a boost when the city made some supportive zoning ordinance changes. (Clegg notes that small-scale farming in the city has much higher per-acre yields than large-scale, commodity production in the nearby counties.) Plans are under way for the city to buy up vacant land near the airport—a measure largely driven by the Federal Aviation Agency's regulatory requirements—and lease it to farmers. That will make 1,258 acres of land available for grazing and crop production.

But what seems to be stirring up the most enthusiasm at city hall these days is a project called Spaulding Ranch. This twenty-acre tract is one of the largest remaining undeveloped parcels in the city, which of course makes it a prime location for just about anything. One proposed use was a new police station, an idea that Clegg characterized as "six acres surrounded by razor wire." Given that the site was formerly used for agriculture, has a perfectly good building suitable for a resident farmer, and is blessed with good topsoil and water rights, community and political weight swung in favor of an educational and demonstration farm. As it stands now, a master plan calls for activities that feature the region's historical agricultural heritage, four acres devoted to chickens and goats, and six to ten acres of crop production.

Projects like these don't simply spring whole cloth from a holy ether. In the case of Boise, a series of small steps, not always precise or intentional, sets the stage for an enduring new idea. As mentioned earlier, Boise's revised urban agriculture ordinance helped defuse any objections to the Spaulding Ranch plan. The regulatory change itself came about through a high level of community involvement in the revision process. Among other provisions, the new ordinance allows for backyard beekeeping ("legalizes bees," as one person put it), the sale of produce from a farm's site, and the carefully prescribed use of farm machinery.

A plan to dispose of the city's organic waste while providing low-cost soil amendments to a local farm has led Boise to truck tons of compostable waste to a place called Twenty Mile South Farm, which is, as anyone who lives in the area knows, twenty miles south of Boise. And in an effort to ensure that as many people as possible benefit from the area's burgeoning local food outlets, the City of Boise sponsors a Double Up Food Bucks program, which doubles the value of food stamps when they are used to buy fresh produce at the city's two farmers' markets. Again, it is not yet commonplace, even in the nation's most progressive cities, for local government to fund such programs.

When I ask Clegg why food has become such a big deal in Boise, she cites a combination of factors that are historical, political, and personal. Accidents of nature and geography are often powerful determinants of who and what we are today, but they are often the first to be forgotten. One group that first settled the Boise area were sheepherders from Spain's Basque region. Since the longitude of the two places is almost identical, it was perhaps logical that the tradition of sheepherding would also flourish in Idaho. Mormon settlers would find fertile ground in the region, bringing not only their agrarian ways but their tradition of self-reliance as well, with growing and canning their own food being part of the Mormon way. The seeds that these early pioneers planted set roots so deep that they are hard to see today, but they do provide a stable foundation for the growth of Boise's food movement.

At a political and policy-making level, where the life span of public recognition is even shorter than it is for a region's history, Clegg gives kudos to Blueprint Boise, the City's comprehensive development plan that was approved in 2011. While city plans like these may provoke skepticism—they are more guidance than law and can easily be ignored—they do represent a formal statement of policy that generally embodies the wishes of the people. As such, it's worth spending a little time with Boise's Blueprint to understand its implications for the local food scene. First off, the language in such plans may be wonky, but it can also suggest an interest in new ideas. The Blueprint uses words and phrases like "sustainability," "preserve and enhance natural resources," "environmental stewardship," and "opportunities for urban agriculture." The plans can tell you what actions the community wants to take: "Support health and social services" and "promote active living and healthy lifestyles." If one were to read between the lines of the Blueprint's professional planners' prose, it might look something like this: *We think it would be a good idea for you to get off your butt and go for a hike or ride a bike. That's the kind of behavior we are encouraging, and we as a city will do what we can to make that an easy choice for you.*

The term "quality of life" will often be used as well. For instance, Boise is becoming a destination for big tech companies like Hewlett-Packard and Micron, not because there's something in Boise's air and water that enables it to build a better laptop, but because a certain quality of life can attract the skilled professionals that those companies need to employ. And as Clegg put it, "those professionals demand a higher quality of life that includes a vibrant community, culture, and *good food*." So, with a nod to a more upscale lifestyle, the Blueprint makes way for mixed-use residential and commercial neighborhoods where restaurants, shops, and brewpubs can be readily accessible throughout the city, not just in one or two downtown clusters.

Many real and potential benefits for food and agriculture exist in the Blueprint, though not always explicitly stated. Yes, the prevalence of more good restaurants and pubs builds markets for locally produced beer (and hop production), hard cider (and orchards), and wine (and vineyards). But terms like "sustainability" and its variations that are sprinkled throughout the document create a favorable environment for numerous food system innovations. Boise's robust approach to composting and a degree of protection for farmland (Clegg hinted at the possibility of additional farmland funding proposals on the table) also help farmers. You'll see references to livestock grazing that the Blueprint makes permissible under specific circumstances within the city's boundaries, as you will find something as simple as an allowance for "shared-use" opportunities at schools that promote school gardens and the use of kitchen facilities after normal school hours. In other words, planning documents like Blueprint Boise establish ground rules that don't say "no!" but say "yes!" to responsible, innovative ideas. Both for-profit and social entrepreneurs can read the Blueprint and see that the city is providing them with an environment favorable to a variety of food activities.

As much as good policy can launch a thousand food and farm projects, and as much as geography and historical patterns of settlement can give a place a favorable gene pool from which to spawn such activities, you can't dismiss the importance of a single person with the right set of attributes appearing at just the right time. Councilwoman Clegg could be just such a person. When I prodded a bit to find out why food was important to her personally, she began to relate stories from her own childhood as well stories about her own children (she has five). Comparing notes, we both realized that we had grown up on a bland 1960s diet that was heavy on processed foods, inspiring a "hunger for food with a different texture, variety, and taste," as she put it. The diversity of Boise's emerging restaurant culture, which includes almost any cuisine you'd find in Berkeley, including Ethiopian and Colombian, excites both her palate and her pride in a place that was known not too long ago for steak and potatoes one day, and potatoes and steak the next.

She also cites the connection between diet and health as a reason for wanting to explore more food options. Having children certainly made her more acutely aware of these connections, so she started them off in the kitchen at an early age. She tells me about one of her boys who, at the age of ten and like all her children, was required to learn how to make a meal or two. Clegg made it easy on him by starting with boxed and canned products like macaroni, fruits, and vegetables. By the time he was sixteen, however, he was placing a shopping list before his mother that included heirloom tomatoes, feta cheese, and a pork loin. Yes, find a person who comes from a solid, homemade stock, add several heaping tablespoons of environmental and health values, season and simmer for many years over the course of motherhood and community activism, and place her in a position of leadership and authority. This will not only be a recipe for success, it will serve thousands.

Evolution of Boise's Food Scene

The farmer-restaurateur relationship is a fragile one, but the quality of that relationship is at the heart of every vital food scene. It's hard if not impossible for the restaurateur to carve out an authentic "eat like a local" niche without the cred that the farmer bestows. For the farmer who spurns the traditional commodity markets or wholesale channels in search of the better margins that direct sales provide, the restaurateur holds out the promise of eternal salvation. But for each to earn the respect and trust of the other is essential, and at times that task is as challenging as going through the stations of the cross.

To explore this relationship, I'm sitting in the Red Feather Lounge, only two blocks from Idaho's state capitol. I'm having a beer with local farmer Tim Sommer, whose face is one of the images found in the large black-and-white farmer posters that adorn the Red Feather's brick walls. Confirming that one photo is indeed him, Tim says with a hint of irony that, "this is a place where we farmers are heroes." I learn early in our conversation that Tim, like most smart farmers I've met, has a well-honed edginess that allows him to confront the adversities of farming as well as cut through the fog that envelops the local food movement. Sometimes, he admits, "you feel like a token," referring to some restaurants and grocers who use your name and farmer credentials to appear more authentic than they really are. "They love the romantic notion of buying 'local' but won't pay what we need, which leaves us marginalized." He reserves a special lash of the whip for some of the big-name organic-food manufacturers and retailers that have moved into Idaho but won't buy from the so-called smaller farmers. "If they say they're buying local, it's a lie."

But like a snake compelled by its nature to release venom, Tim calms down and relaxes his coils. Casting his eyes about the crowded restaurant owned by one of Boise's pioneering chefs, David Crick, he says, "Dave's the truth . . . he makes it work." There's nothing grudging in this praise. It's heartfelt but speaks to the frisson that often exists between entrepreneurial spirits who inhabit both ends of the food chain. If nothing else, Tim's affirmation of Crick's sincerity is itself a testament to how vexing the job of closing the gaps between farmer, restaurateur, and eater have become. Tim tells me there are ten genuine farm-to-table restaurants in Boise, but worried that he's getting too warm and fuzzy, he qualifies the number by asserting that it does not include "the two that are greenwashers."

The complexity of Tim's journey speaks to his persistence as a farmer, which might sometimes be mistaken for pigheadedness. Though he had early roots in farming, Tim tried his hand in the corporate world, where he worked in marketing. Fueled by a desire to return to farming, he eventually found himself running 1,800 head of cattle in Idaho, a number that sounds impressive to the non-farmer or non-rancher but is in fact minuscule in the American world of livestock feedlots dominated by megacorporations like Iowa Beef. Ultimately unable to compete, Tim put his marketing hat back on to discover that herbs and microgreens were a far more profitable niche than beef. "Downsizing" from raising 1,500-pound animals to raising plants that are sold fresh by the ounce may seem almost *Alice in Wonderland* freakishly up and down, but when the former earns you barely one dollar per pound on a really good day, and the latter grosses twenty dollars per pound, then maybe there is something special in those mushrooms after all.

This massive switch can't be attributed entirely to Tim's shrewdness in reading market signals. Making a comment I found common in Boise,

Tim said, "We're not all Vermont, and our farmers' idea of getting 'wild and crazy' is growing garlic!" Guy Hand had told me earlier that Boise is a meat-and-potatoes kind of place, and as David Crick would say later, "When it comes to our food scene, we're not Portland [Oregon]." There is a collective acknowledgment of their reality as well as a mild inferiority complex. Being market savvy is a necessary part of the business-development process. Looking outward to America's iconic food and farm places can inspire you to find your own identity, or it can drive you to despair. How do you change the direction of food, farming, and people when their tastes haven't progressed much beyond Conestoga days?

It might be counterintuitive for most Idahoans to look to government as a force for change, but the Idaho State Department of Agriculture (ISDA) stepped up in the early 1990s with its own organic certification program. It's become so popular that the ISDA had to temporarily limit the program to the current four hundred farmers now participating. To interest a department that rarely looked beyond the state's commodity agricultural businesses, Tim called upon the services of his brother-in-law, who was an Idaho state senator at the time. That was the political leverage he needed to convince the state to establish organic certification guidelines and inspection services.

But without consumer demand, good state agricultural policy and hundreds of local and organic farmers are all dressed up with nowhere to go. The day after Tim's impassioned interview with me, I've moved only one hundred feet from the Red Feather Lounge to the other side of the same building, known as the Bittercreek Alehouse. I'm sipping a tasty Moon Dog Red Ale, brewed in Boise, waiting for the owner of both establishments, David Crick, to arrive. Wearing glasses that make him appear bookish, he sits down at my booth wearing a black, insignia-less ball cap pulled down so low on his face that I have to bend over to look up into his eyes.

David is a serious, mission-driven guy who's also open and affable. He tells me he started in the food world as a "beer guy" who earned his BS in Munich, Germany (BS as in "brewing science" degree). But Dave's love of culture and place drew him deeper into the culinary life. "What's your culinary identity?" is the question he asks of himself and other restaurateurs, not to determine so much how you're listed in local restaurant guides, but to confront the very reason for your existence. It's not just that chefs should go on the occasional pilgrimage to find their soul, but as David sees it, a strong identity between a place and cuisine equals economic value. "What's the most expensive farmland in the world?" he asks me. "The Loire Valley in France, not because their wine is necessarily the best wine in the world, but because it commands a high price due to its Loire Valley identity."

It is the same self-reinforcing logic that David applies to his pursuit of identity and value for Boise's food scene. In what he refers to as "geo-tourism"—an enlightened traveler, the geo-tourist chooses destinations for their perceived geographical, historical, and cultural attributes—a strong connection between local farms and restaurants that make a unique Boise statement will, economically speaking, raise all ships. With menu offerings that are strong on Idaho trout, lamb, and vegetables (including potatoes, of course), and a cellar and taps slanted toward Idaho wine, beer, and cider, the Red Feather Lounge and Bittercreek Alehouse seem to have found the path to prosperity. Compared to when they started in 2002, David says Red Feather–Bittercreek have tripled their sales. "I never imagined the market we'd have now—so many people who care about food!"

A local food identity is strengthened by the synergy created between multiple outlets and events; foodie vectors, you might say, emanating from numerous sources, shooting in untold directions, intersecting at unpredictable intervals. For instance, David and Tim both acknowledge the power and proximity of the Boise farmers' market, located only a couple of blocks from Red Feather. They praise Janie Burns for her numerous creations, including "Tomato Tuesday." And they both agreed that the number of authentic farm-to-table restaurants was exactly ten.

But the synergy among food spaces is further reinforced by the energy of events not overtly food related. Such is the case with Boise's Treefort Music Fest, which is held for several days at the end of March. Dozens of bands and other arts performers, children's activities, yoga gatherings, and film screenings fill Boise's downtown streets just as spring's warm breath is thawing everyone's spirits. Food and beverage, however, run through this lively celebration in somewhat surprising and slightly understated ways. About a dozen of Treefort's major sponsors are food and beverage companies or organizations including the Boise Food Co-Op, Bittercreek Alehouse, and the Modern Hotel and Bar—all very local, all very "down home." There is a health focus as well. In addition to the yoga program, there is a large presence from St. Luke's Children's Hospital and an anti-tobacco organization called Project Filter. Health, local food, and a unique Boise vibe are all central to the celebration. Of course, anyone attending fairs and local festivals is used to seeing food, but the local identity is often drowned by a near endless string of Coca-Cola, Burger King, and Subway vendors.

The progress people make always feels limited by how far they still have to go rather than how far they've come. "We must meet our community where they are at," says David, "so we make a really good local lamb burgers and fries." But doesn't that market manacle hold you back? In his less stoical moments, he admits, "we [Boise's culinary community] don't know where we're going. We're still in an early exploratory phase." In spite of the barriers that confront the farmer–local buyer–consumer interface described by Tim Sommers ("People around here think they're getting local food at Trader Joe's"), an unassailable solidarity exists in the local food community. In the winter of 2017, the Boise region experienced record snowfalls that, among other calamities, caused several of Tim's greenhouses to collapse. "The community kicked in thirty thousand dollars to help me rebuild," Tim told me. You could say there's a simmering kind of optimism afoot when you hear from restaurateurs that farmers are learning lessons that make their crop selection and product-handling methods more desirable to chefs. Culinary confidence in itself—pushing back against the "Who are we?" identity demons and the lurking shadows of Vermont and Portland—is also emerging. As David said, "Boise used to chase its chefs away," meaning that anyone with an ounce of imagination was tagged as some kind of rapacious parvenu. Today, while not yet placed on pedestals, they are sure getting lots of positive feedback.

The strengths are in the ties that bind. The weaknesses are in a dominant food system that doesn't recognize the importance of those ties, or of community, or even the simple notion that hard struggle should be rewarded. Tim's farm won an award from a state farming organization, but he can't generate sufficient revenues to pay his workers a living wage, which is a source of frustration to him. Without the well-paying job his wife, Tamara, holds at Hewlett-Packard, the farm's financial challenges might not be tolerable. "She gives me tractor parts for my birthday and Christmas presents," he tells me with a guilty grin. And he's done his share of policy work to level the playing field between large commodity farms and smaller specialty operations like his, but grows furious when he acknowledges the lion's share of state and federal funding still finds its way to Big Ag.

On the other side of the building from where Tim shares his story, David Crick tells me he'll soon be opening a taco bar next door using local feed corn that the restaurant will grind itself. This business confidence is buoyed by the collaboration that takes place among his fellow restaurateurs. They have realized that cooperation is a safer bet than competition, and that they'll learn to swim together or sink alone. But David readily acknowledges his debt to farmers. Shaking his head slowly side to side and casting his eyes downward, he says, "My friends who farm still struggle, and that defeats me every day."

Food Security

As much as local IPAs and heirloom tomatoes improve my quality of life, they don't do a lot to stem food insecurity. That is why the Summit on Idaho Hunger & Food Security has held its biennial conference for the past twelve years. In 2016, the one-day event delved into six broad topics ranging from anti-hunger advocacy to childhood nutrition to, yes, local food systems, which, interestingly, drew the most people out of the crowd of two hundred. Protecting the programs that protect Idaho's most vulnerable citizens, (that is, SNAP and child nutrition recipients), and recognizing the multiple values associated with local food are a high priority for a small but passionate crowd of Idaho food activists. Having decided to poke the bear, keynote speaker and then USDA Under Secretary Kevin Concannon told the audience we must have a higher minimum wage to reduce hunger, an idea that, had it traveled much beyond the conference center, would have been enough to mobilize the Idaho militia. To make the link between local food and food security, Concannon proudly noted that 7,000 of the nation's approximately 8,500 farmers' markets accept SNAP.

～

As I was listening to the talks, I couldn't help but think of Wilder, Idaho, a town that I visited on the previous day's farm country tour. Nestled in the middle of ever-expanding hopyards and vineyards, Wilder is 76 percent Hispanic, has a 32 percent poverty rate, and 94 percent of its schoolchildren qualify for free and reduced-price lunch (49 percent is the state average). In short, Wilder is one of the poorest towns in Idaho, and its residents are largely agricultural workers. Wilder's residents are the foundation of Idaho's booming farm economy, yet their children may never have the chance to leave the fields that literally surround them. As of now, their critical lifelines are federal food programs.

But food programs may not be Wilder's first worry. If President Trump follows through on his draconian plan to deport undocumented immigrants, Idaho's Hispanic community and agricultural businesses would suffer disproportionately to the rest of the nation. According to the *Idaho Statesman* (November 12, 2016), one-fourth of the state's agricultural workforce could be lost, and even worse, children could be separated from their parents.

The Connection

Residents of Wilder may also work at the J. R. Simplot plant not more than thirty minutes away. But due to a technology overhaul, the potato processing plant went from about 1,000 workers to 185, leaving redundant workers with nothing but seasonal farmwork. Ironically, the good food economy may begin to replace the not-so-good food economy. Chobani Greek Yogurt opened a new plant in 2012 in Twin Falls, Idaho, with the goal of employing five hundred people. (It did vacuum up about $55 million in public subsidies in the process.) Hot on Chobani's heels is the organic snack food giant Clif Bar, which is opening a $90 million facility, also in Twin Falls, that will employ 250 workers.

Food security advocates are joining forces with local foodies in the form of the Double Up Food Bucks program that is connecting SNAP recipients to thirteen farmers' markets around the state. Over, thirty-five thousand Ada County residents received about $48 million in SNAP benefits in 2016, or about 20 percent of all such benefits in the state. When combined with adjoining Canyon County's thirty-two thousand SNAP recipients, this small section of Southwestern Idaho accounted for nearly 40 percent of all SNAP beneficiaries. Farm-to-school programs, lots of food and nutrition education from the University of Idaho Extension Service, and innovative gardening programs are bringing more of the state's food vectors into alignment.

But perhaps the most telling connection was the hunger summit itself. By making the local food system a conference focus, bridges were built between different elements of Idaho's food movement. As Janie Burns observed, "I suppose the best way to describe food work in Idaho is to compare it to a quilt. We are each still making our own little blocks and squares. Occasionally, we get to make new squares and even sew two together. [The hunger summit] was a great start to that effort."

Boise is a place that builds bridges between like-minded interests at the same time that it progressively and even aggressively asserts its values in sometimes unfriendly terrain. Though it keeps looking over its shoulder at that Big Bad Conservative Bear, it pushes ahead with the goal of becoming a modern city with a small-town heart. Bridges between farmers and restaurateurs, environmental and farming interests, city hall and the people, hunger programs and farmers, and other elements of the food system are making Boise a problem-solving kind of place. At the same time, it owns up to its challenges honestly and courageously.

CHAPTER 4
Sitka, Alaska

We're skimming at full speed across the calm gray waters of Sitka Bay in a 40-horsepower open skiff. Any speed on water feels fast when there's no enclosure to break the wind, and the same can be said for the cold. The wind on this overcast July day in Southeast Alaska, with the thermometer barely reaching 60 degrees, has set my bones to rattling. Having had passengers like me before, Andrea Fraga, the boat's pilot and the farmer to whose farm we're riding, handed me a heavy, insulated jacket that I quickly became friends with.

Between her aviator sunglasses and chestnut brown hair blowing straight back, Andrea looks every inch the New Mexico cowgirl coolly guiding a galloping colt across an open range. Instead of the occasional antelope, however, we're passing sea lions, bald eagles, and sprawling carpets of kelp that cling to scattered outcroppings of rocks. Her Welsh corgi, Abbey, is crouched low in the hull, eyes closed to the wind, as is our companion passenger and fellow Sitkan farmer, Laura Schmidt. Together, we're headed to Andrea's Middle Island Garden, which I am told is out there somewhere on the horizon that is so hopelessly cluttered with islands that I can't possibly tell which one is the "middle."

The boat's gunnels barely kiss the dock as Andrea snuggles the outboard into place. I'm staring straight up at a steep embankment from which towering stands of Sitka spruce, yellow cedar, and western hemlock ascend. I'm already asking myself how in God's good name could there be a farm out here. But almost by magic, stone steps tucked into the hillside as if they'd been there a thousand years appear, easing my way into the rain forest. Passing by moss-encrusted tree trunks, stacks of firewood, and a workshop so adorable it looks as if it were built by a team of gnome craftsmen, I notice the sky reappearing overhead, and I'm suddenly gazing upon the better part of Middle Island Garden.

Based on size, Andrea's "farm" may provide one of the more underwhelming agricultural experiences you'll ever have. Based on the tenacity required to carve a few thousand square feet of production space out of the wilderness, the growing area conjures up the mythical feats of Paul Bunyan. Based on density of planting, output per square foot, and the sheer vitality of the plants, you might as well be standing in the Garden of Eden. Over twelve hundred garlic plants align themselves with perfect symmetry the length of three beds. Robust pea vines climb as strong and high as the animated ones in "Jack and Beanstalk." Yes, there are the legendary Alaskan cabbages with six-foot wing spans, but there are also blackberries, kale, beets, sunchokes, hardy kiwi, and the made-for-short-growing-seasons William's Pride apple trees. Red currants fill in the shadier spots while columbines accent the sunnier borders. When I jokingly ask Andrea if she's getting such spectacular results by feeding her plants some noxious chemical fertilizer banned in the Lower 48, she utters just one word: "Kelp."

Up until recently, she had sought out nearby, soil-enriching kelp in the early spring, when the herrings came to her inlet to spawn. The fertilized roe found their way into the kelp, which gave her seaweed a nutrient boost. This bonus came at a cost, as she discovered one night when she was about to retire. Not having indoor toilet facilities in an otherwise beautiful house that she and her partner, Kaleb, built, Andrea found her usual outdoor spot to relieve herself not far from the day's harvest of roe-saturated kelp. Staring back at her was a large brown bear snarfing up as much roe as it could. After spotlights, foghorns, banging pots, and the threat of a deer rifle, the bear retreated, but Andrea resolved henceforth to forgo the roe "bonus."

The Little Town That Could

It can be hard enough living in a place where there are critters that occupy a rung above you in the food chain. It's even harder when your entire community is at the end of the national food chain and dependent on semiweekly barge shipments from Seattle for 95 percent of your food. This vulnerability became immediately obvious to me when I arrived at Sitka's Saturday morning farmers' market at ten thirty to buy some produce. Though it had just opened at ten o'clock, the stalls were nearly empty. I managed to grab a head of lettuce (courtesy of Laura Schmidt, who sold me her last one) and a bunch of beach asparagus about which I knew nothing. When I asked Andrea, who had one bunch of garlic scapes left, what her annual gross sales were, I was shocked to hear that she could produce that much food off three thousand square feet, but humbled when I realized what a small percentage of the community's need her sales and those of her few fellow farmers represented.

Sitka's insecure food position is partially offset by the fact that its nine thousand residents occupy a narrow strip of land that is surrounded by unparalleled natural bounty and beauty. On one side, the ocean appears to offer an endless quantity of marine species such as salmon, halibut, herring roe, and rockfish. On the forest and mountain side, which in some places descends very steeply to barely a half mile from the ocean, game is available to hunt, and plants and berries to gather. Based on a food survey done by the Sitka Local Foods Network (SLFN), 48 percent of Sitkans access fish and game through hunting and fishing (another 24 percent receive subsistence food—fished, hunted, or gathered—from others as gifts or donations), and 57 percent eat fish or game several times a week. These high numbers reflect several factors, including the simple fact that wild food is so abundant, food purchased at stores is so expensive, Alaskan residents are entitled to harvest wild food for subsistence purposes (its cost is free or very low, assuming you don't need a boat), and perhaps most important, Native Alaskans have always relied on wild food—long before there were grocery stores, food barges, or food stamps.

Sitka is one of the most expensive places in the United States to buy food. Not only are food prices 35 percent higher than the US mainland average, they are 10 to 21 percent higher than all but the most remote Alaskan towns. People make a mighty effort to grow some of their own, but minuscule amounts of even partially flat land and stony soils conspire against the most tenacious gardener. I was to learn during a week of research in Sitka that small things like herring roe matter, and that big things like food cannot be taken for granted. Over 850 miles by air from Seattle and even farther by sea, Sitka is not accessible to the mainland by road. And when the food barge is delayed by bad weather and logistical malfunctions, which is often, terms like "food insecurity" as well as "traditional and subsistence foods" take on more profound meanings.

But I would learn one more thing about Sitka that would put its strengths and weaknesses into perspective: the place has an uncommon sense of community that keeps a watchful eye on its food security and pushes and pulls relentlessly to find solutions to difficult challenges. Like the childhood tale of the little train pushing with all its might up a steep grade, Sitka is the little town that could. None of which is to say, of course, that it suffers quietly, enduring long, subarctic nights with nothing but dried strips of salmon to gnaw on. Celebration of place and food abound, informed by a proximity to forests, to the ocean, to

Native traditions, and even to mundane things like seaweed. Great coffee shops, brewpubs, and some darn good chefs have turned this watery location into a place that will keep most demanding foodies happy. It is a place where the men under forty have ruddy, seawater-scrubbed cheeks, scruffy beards, and ball caps with fishing logos pulled down tight over their heads. It's a place where the women know how to gut and fillet a seven-pound salmon, aim and shoot a rifle, field-dress a deer, and prepare the best seafood quiche you'll ever eat. And it's a place where people pull together for the common good.

A Collective Blessing

I'm sitting in the backseat of Keith Nyitray's eighteen-year-old Ford Escape as he gives me a tour of "greater" Sitka. It's not that I have some kind of VIP status that puts Keith in the chauffeur position, it's more that his front passenger door is broken and all the other seats are occupied with documents and products for the Sitka Food Co-op, which Keith manages. The tour doesn't take long. It's one road that goes seven miles south from downtown, and the same road that goes seven miles north. They both dead-end after passing Sitka's three small grocery stores, fish-processing plants, the tourist cruise ship terminal, a few microfarms, the Baranof Island Brewing Company, a trailer park, chocolate factory, fish hatchery, and a hodgepodge of marine- and auto-repair businesses.

Keith is tall, wiry, and energetic beyond his fifty-nine years, and reminds me of the "co-opers" I knew in my early days who were so smitten with managing small co-ops that they worked 24-7 for what amounted to a subminimum wage. He tells me that his compensation is only a little more than Alaska's minimum wage of $9.84 per hour, and he often "eats" his overtime. We end up at the Mean Queen, a restaurant and bar that doesn't quite qualify as a dive—there are a couple of such smoky establishments in town—but barely rises to the level of mediocre. Mary Magnuson is the proprietress, who seems neither mean nor particularly regal, but presides over the noisy venue with enough authority to maintain order. Should things ever get out of hand, my assumption is that she would pull a baseball bat out from under the bar.

As revved up as he is, Keith manages the co-op prudently and professionally, resisting the pressure to expand as fast as possible. Currently there are 230 family members, and because, according to Keith, the average co-op price is 26 percent lower than the town's grocery stores, the demand to grow is constant. Currently, the co-op operates two days a month out of Harrigan Centennial Hall, a waterfront community center. All member orders are placed online, which makes it quite easy for Keith to compile them and place orders with wholesalers that are located on the mainland. (On two occasions when I was interviewing Keith, he was giving one-on-one ordering tutorials for new members.) All in all, the co-op is providing 5.5 tons of food each month with total annual sales valued at $500,000.

Sitka doesn't have a Walmart or a Sam's Club. Competition among the small grocery stores is not sufficient to keep food prices down, and they do not possess large buying or storage capacity. On a small scale, what the co-op is doing is pooling the buying power of its members to secure the discounts associated with larger-scale buying. But its smallness, which is a function of not having a permanent facility, is a drawback.

"Given Sitka's economic trends, we know that the co-op will continue to grow at a substantial rate. We need a permanent, store-like space that will help us meet the need," Keith told me. Up until the fall of 2018, Keith and other co-opers thought their dreams for a facility of their very own would come true. The First Presbyterian Church, which had ministered to the Sitka community for one hundred years, held its last service that July. Since it was also housing a variety of community services, including a community kitchen, Keith saw the decommissioned church as a perfect space for an expanded co-op as well as a potential community food center. But unexpected snafus emerged, sinking the deal to the chagrin of all involved.

In a place like Sitka, where nothing comes easy, setbacks are part of the territory. Hard-driving social entrepreneurs like Keith and private entrepreneurs like Andrea know how to roll with the punches, but true grit is never enough. Without community support—some kind of collective blessing, as it were—the innovation and sweat that flow from individual creativity are not nurtured, often leaving good ideas flailing in the wind. In Sitka, there is an institutional bridge of sorts that raises up good ideas, connects them to the community, and incubates them until they are able to stand on their own. That process was itself the brainchild of the Southeast Alaska Regional Health Consortium (SEARHC), which started the annual Sitka Health Summit as a way to bring the community together around a broadly defined agenda to promote health.

Doug Osborn is the Director of Health Promotion for the Sitka Community Hospital, and the primary mover and shaker behind the health summit, which is actually a coalition of Sitka health agencies and organizations. He tells me that Sitka is perhaps slightly healthier, at least statistically, than other Alaskan communities, but substance abuse, alcoholism, and diabetes are serious problems for the community. Doug said that, "less than one-quarter of the population are getting the recommended five a day of fruits and vegetables."

He attributes Sitka's generally better health profile to several things, including its more liberal political attitudes, higher education levels, and a reasonably diverse economy that's based on tourism, health care, seafood, and education. But the big thing that stands out for him, as well as just about everyone else I met in Sitka is social capital, that "glue" that holds people together, usually for the purpose of getting something done that they couldn't do by themselves.

The centerpiece of the summit, and where you'll find social capital bursting at the seams, is "Planning Day." That's when up to one hundred citizens meet, listen to ideas for community improvement, and after hearing out numerous proposals, select two or three ideas for support. As Doug told me, food is among the community's top concerns. Out of the twenty initiatives selected by the summit since its start in 2007, about half were related to food, including a composting project, citywide fruit-tree planting, a community kitchen, large gardens, the farmers' market, a Fish to School project, and even a community food assessment.

By the end of Planning Day, the initiatives are selected and groups are formed to shepherd them to success. Each initiative group receives start-up funds (a modest amount of perhaps $2,000 each) as well as support from the Sitka Health Summit. Since 2007, the vast majority of the initiatives were characterized as highly successful, though a handful have failed or simply never got off the ground. Win or lose, the event brings people together to launch a number of small but transformative projects that have probably touched every member of the community.

The health summit is not the only time when the community comes together to build their common wealth. Voluntarism abounds, sometimes with so much energy that it feels like too many atoms colliding in too small a space. According to Keith, there are 123 nonprofit organizations in Sitka, which for a town of nine thousand people is a lot, and that's not counting houses of faith and various other civic organizations, such as Kiwanis. By law, each nonprofit must have a board of directors. In a town like Sitka, with so much to do and not enough money to pay for the necessary staff, board members must often do some of the program work. Several people I spoke with told me their organization's work was often limited by a lack of volunteers to fill seats on the board. This is a common problem in rural areas and small towns, where the same people are often tapped to do too much work until they find themselves emotionally tapped out.

The Sea

"I can drop a line in the water and catch a rockfish for dinner. That's how amazing this place is!" is how Gary Downie Jr., a fisherman and ecotour boat operator, talks about his hometown. We're headed out across Sitka Bay to Redoubt, where people are supposedly hauling in their household allocation of twenty-five sockeye salmon in fifteen minutes or less. Gary's boat is bigger than Andrea's, and is powered by twin 40-horsepower outboards, so we're cruising at a pretty good clip. More important, his boat is partially enclosed, which means I don't have to fake how warm I am.

When I ask Gary why Sitka is so special, other than easy access to "takeout of the sea" food, he says, "I'm thirty-seven and I've been here thirty-seven years. My family has been here since 1936. I always tell people Sitka is magic." Worried that I'm getting a little bit of the usual charter boat captain palaver that tourists often hear, I press him for details. He doesn't disappoint. "There's a feeling of health—people hike a lot. If you're smart about your diet and work hard, you can get what you need from the ocean and the forest." His girlfriend is a "raw foodist," he tells me, and he proudly proclaims his status as a "card-carrying member" of the Sitka Food Co-op, whose virtues—"amazing food and low prices"—he extols to no end.

The leaden sky that has accompanied me for the past three days has lifted, unveiling jagged, treeless mountain peaks whose crevasses are still filled with snow. We're moving deeper into the bay as Gary finds channels between islands that I don't see until the very last minute. Fishing boats are anchored or moving slowly as they troll for salmon. We stop and observe one boat that is hauling in a gill net, a long net pulled behind the boat that catches the fish by the gills, making them easy to remove once on board. He tells me about what species of salmon are supposed to run when and where—king, coho, sockeye, red, and chum. There's life and signs of prosperity all around us; people are catching fish and making a livelihood, but a slightly sorrowful tone creeps into Gary's otherwise spirited chatter. "This is a bad year for king salmon," he tells me, shaking his head. "I feel like things are changing. There's a fisherman we all know who's so good that we all say, 'He thinks like a fish.' Even he's not catching much right now."

His explanations are a litany of everything I've heard before and then some. "The Blob," as Gary refers to it, is a large warm water mass off the Alaskan coast that affects the larger marine habitat. The "stream" that so much sea life, from herrings to humpbacks, circulates in is a massive ocean current that moves counterclockwise along the Southeast Alaska coast, then west along the southern coast all the way out to the Aleutian Islands, then south to Hawaii, where it turns east and back to Alaska. The Blob and other manifestations of global warming could be affecting this system.

But in what has reached the level of universal chant, he suggests that the culprit is overfishing. "Fishermen don't want to hear bad news, which is why they'll resist change. I used to be a commercial fisherman," he reminds me, "but now I'm doing wildlife and environmental tours—the eco-friendly thing—because I'm concerned." When I ask him to be more specific, he says, "The ocean used to be lit up blue and green during the spring herring run. This place was hammered by herring. Now it's not." He looks wistfully out over the water and says, "The Tlingit elders will tell you what it used to be like—you could practically walk across the bay on the backs of herring. What the fuck is going on?"

There's no doubt that fishing is an integral part of just about everything in Sitka. Its people are employed throughout the fishing industry, seafood is a staple in the diet unlike just about anywhere else in the Lower 48, and its fishing fleet of over five hundred boats is a virtual armada. For the Sitka Tribe, fish aren't just a part of their weekly meal plan; they are a traditional food that's fused to their spiritual life and an underpinning of their cultural survival.

Yet the breaking story here is that there are cracks in the foundation. The fishing industry is a part of a global commodity market, which means that fishermen are price takers, not price makers. Climate change is a vast though still vaguely unpredictable maelstrom that has the potential to take everyone down. The Native Alaskans see the quantities of their traditional foods like salmon and herring roe taking a nosedive. And if you can't fish or don't own a boat, there is no retail outlet in Sitka dedicated to seafood where one can buy retail quantities of fish at reasonable prices.

"Sitka only exists because of global demand," is how Nicholaas "Nic" Mink, founder of Sitka Salmon Shares put it. Nic, who is also a professor of natural resources at Knox College in Galesburg, Illinois, where he splits his time with Sitka, has been studying the fisheries and their impact on communities for most of his career. He's referring to what amounts to an escalating surge in the world's hunger for fish protein. As Nic sees it, Alaska's fisheries are part of a "colonial food system because most of the catch is going to Asia." The Alaskan fisheries are among the best managed in the world, and a state law (instigated by a state legislator from Sitka) even bans fish farming in Alaskan waters. While these actions protect Sitka's $150 million fishing industry, they can't control prices that are set globally, nor can they rein in the rough climate change beast now slouching toward Alaska. Sitka's fishermen are paid at rates subject to global market forces, not local, wild-caught, retail rates. The premium price of thirty dollars a pound for wild-caught salmon that I pay at Whole Foods is not equitably redistributed down to the local fisherman.

In light of all these forces, Nic Mink set out to put fishermen at the center of the marine food system chain while also attempting to get better control over fish quality and the impact on the environment. Salmon Shares was started in 2010 as a for-profit corporation whose primary shareholders are fishermen. The original numbers were small but have reached forty independent fishermen-owners today. Nic refers to them as "artisanal hook-and-line fishermen" who use prescribed practices to ensure the least damage to the fish and the best on-board handling to ensure the highest quality.

Salmon Shares operates its own small fish processing plant that employs forty people at the peak of the season. I took a tour where I experienced the heart-stopping chill of a freezer at negative 80 degrees Fahrenheit. The faster a fish can be moved from the sea to a freezer—for Salmon Share's fishermen, that's a maximum of four days—and the faster it can be frozen—for this freezer, that's one inch of fish thickness an hour—the less damage there is to cell structure. About a dozen men were packing and unpacking fiber totes with whole, gutted fish onto tables where they were cut, trimmed, and filleted before going into the freezer. Once frozen, they are loaded back into the totes, which are loaded into a mobile freezer unit that is kept at 10 below. Those units are shipped by barge to Seattle and then shipped to Galesburg, Illinois, by truck, where the fillets are individually Cryovac packed for distribution to Salmon Shares' six thousand customers in Illinois and Wisconsin. The bottom line: customers are paying a little less than they would for the same quality at Whole Foods, fishermen are making 15 to 20 percent more than selling into conventional wholesale channels, and forty full- and part-time jobs are created.

But perhaps there's an additional benefit that's derived from those six thousand (and growing) members who receive and pay attention to the personal stories of the fishermen as well as information about what's going on in the fisheries. As Nic put it, "We can't keep up [with changes in the oceans]—the fisheries are being remade before our eyes!" He cites one species, Pacific cod, which has all but disappeared as a result of climate change. The iconic Copper River salmon run (a fish I spent forty dollars a pound for in the spring of 2017 as a special treat) had been shut down since mid-June. The residents of Sitka see these things happening before their eyes every day. Sharing the stories of the sea and its inhabitants with more landbound people is part of what Salmon Shares is all about.

There is one place where Sitkans receive a direct benefit from the sea without having to catch fish themselves, and that's in the schools. In a town where more than half the students qualify for free or reduced-price meals, the nonprofit Sitka Conservation Society (SCS) worked to establish what is probably the first and certainly one of the nation's few Fish to School programs. I caught up with Mary Jo Michalski ("Chef Jo") at the Jo's Downtown Dawgs cart she runs in the summer when she's not overseeing Sitka's School Food Service Program. As I was clutching a reindeer sausage "dawg" smothered in sauce and sauerkraut that was big enough to sustain two men at sea for a week, she told me that she had been noticing more kids coming to school hungry. So, in addition to serving 600 lunches a day, she's added 150 breakfasts to give lower-income kids the energy they need to learn. She also told me she wasn't happy with the healthfulness of the meals that were being served, which led to changing up the menu to increase nutritional content. This was where the fish came in.

Almost any school district in the United States would be hard-pressed to come up with enough extra cash to purchase fresh, "right off the boat" salmon. But when millions of pounds are being landed only blocks away from the school kitchen, one would think there would be a way. With the assistance of the SCS, donated fish would be delivered to the schools to create a fish entrée every Wednesday. Chef Jo was thrilled with this option and set to work creating a host of kid-friendly fish dishes, including some terrific fish chowder that turned into a school favorite.

But Fish to School is an example of a good idea that butts up against the realities of changing fisheries. Sitka should be the most logical place in the world to use fish to nourish children. Now it appears to be an early victim of declining fish runs. According to Chef Jo, she'll be able to offer local fish only every other week because the fishermen cannot donate as much. Her dilemma raises a thorny ethical question that we will all be grappling with in the future: Will our kids (you can substitute the poor, people of color, the elderly) become the first ones sacrificed to global warming?

Traditional Food and the First People

Totem poles have been a vital part of the Native Tlingit oral tradition in Southeast Alaska. About a decade ago, the ancient medium was "reinvented" to communicate messages of health and wellness on the grounds of Sitka's SEARHC Community Health Services center. It is known as the Wellbriety Pole and includes traditional images like the raven, but also carvings of a shaman and medicine woman that reference issues of alcoholism, substance abuse, diabetes, and cancer. Reams of statistics are not required to underscore the seriousness of these public health threats, to which we can now add climate change and overfishing. They are easily discernible in the image of a medicine woman with a tear rolling down her cheek.

I learned more about the cause of her sadness during my time in Sitka. I discovered that traditional foods like salmon, herring roe, deer, and beach asparagus take on profound meanings that are rarely imagined in non-Native North America. As indicated by the SLFN survey, the vast majority of Sitkans consume a lot of fish, game, and wild forage foods. But for the Tlingit and other Native people who comprise the four thousand citizens of the Sitka Tribe (2,500 live in Sitka), these subsistence foods are an integral part of their cultural tradition. The region's land and waters are the provenance not only of the tribe's sustenance, but also its soul and spirit. Unfortunately, the same survey revealed that 60 percent of the tribe's members were not able to consume as much of their traditional food as they want.

The biggest threat to traditional foods appears to come from the $5 billion Alaska seafood industry. Without traditional foods, Native culture is weakened and individual health compromised. Compared to non-Hispanic white people, American Indians and Alaska Natives are 2.3 times more likely to be diagnosed with diabetes, and their youth are *9 times* more likely to have diagnosed type 2 diabetes (US Department of Health and Human Services, 2012).

While Alaskans, including state government, generally acknowledge that Native people hold a certain cultural primacy, a "first claim," as it were, to the region's bounty, it doesn't mean that Natives are exempt from navigating the confusing maze of federal, state, and private land jurisdictions that promulgate regulations governing where, what, when, how, and how much game and fish can be harvested.

Wild Catch

The Sitka Tribe's administrative offices are tucked in between harbor docks and fish-processing plants. Bald eagles circling immediately overhead pursuing abundant fish scraps are nearly as prevalent as pigeons in Central Park picking up bread crumbs. On my way into the building, I pass a totem pole depicting families and health. I'm here to see Jeff Feldpausch, the director of the tribe's Natural Resource Department, who has run the traditional-foods program for fourteen years while vigorously advocating for the protection of those foods. I learn quickly that his knowledge of marine fisheries is based on science, practice, and perhaps most important, local traditional knowledge.

Among the tribe's several major projects is its own research station called Southeast Alaska Tribal Ocean Research (SEATOR). It is a tribal government partnership that was set up to monitor ocean acidification and toxins produced by algal blooms that find their way into mollusks. Ocean acidification has increased 30 percent over the last three hundred years due to an increase in atmospheric carbon. According to Jeff, "It is a serious threat to Southeast Alaska because of our reliance on healthy fisheries and access to marine resources." From among the species they have studied, the data shows decreased calcification, fish growth, reproduction, and survival.

"We've seen a decline in the wild catch, not just for us, but across the board for all harvesters," Jeff tells me. Expressing frustration with the Alaska Board of Fisheries for failing to lower catch limits, he says, "We've exhausted all our avenues. We're considering other approaches including . . ." He paused at that point, presumably deciding not to tip the tribe's hand.

But as much as the tribe advocates for the protection of subsistence food, it does what it can to gather food for its people. Over the past year, Jeff's department has harvested about twenty thousand pounds of game and seafood that is distributed first to the tribe's elders, and then to others based on availability.

While twenty thousand pounds may sound like a lot of food to those of us who don't rely on subsistence harvesting, it doesn't come close to meeting the needs. Keep in mind that subsistence food in Alaska is only 1 percent of the entire wild harvest, with 98 percent—mostly seafood— caught by commercial harvesters who ship it out of Alaska.

One small species that threatens to further turn up the heat between the Sitka Tribe and State of Alaska is the lowly herring and its roe. Echoing the charter boat operator Gary Downie, Jeff said, "Herring is a critical forage fish for our marine ecosystem—a foundation and bell-wether species—but right now, we're seeing the worst herring roe year since 2002. Our tribe's elders don't remember seeing such limited spawning." According to Alaska's Department of Fish and Game, only 107,000 pounds of roe were harvested in 2015. Harvest figures for 2018 are likely to be lower. Its estimate of how much roe is necessary to meet the region's subsistence needs is between 136,000 and 227,000 pounds.

Based on an ethnographic study conducted by Portland State University of nearly two hundred Sitka Tribal members with "local and traditional knowledge of herring populations," present herring stocks are being managed in a "depleted status" that represents a fraction of their historical abundance. It concluded that lower rates of herrings and roe threaten "biodiversity and regional marine food webs" and the cultural life of the region's Native people. According to Harold Marin, one interviewee from the study, "Herring are just so important to the total food chain. . . . They feed everything. . . . We didn't like the idea of commercial fishermen coming in and taking them on a large scale."

Mr. Marin may have identified the crux of the problem: the Japanese market for roe, which they call *Kazunoko*. The Native method of harvesting roe is simply to place hemlock boughs just below low tide, where the herring spawn. The boughs are then retrieved and the roe removed; the fish is never touched. Commercial fishermen use seine nets to haul in huge quantities of herrings. They don't distinguish between male and female or their respective sizes. Roe sacs are stripped from the fish cavity, and the dead fish are ground into fertilizer, fish oil, and feed for salmon farms, which, ironically are banned in Alaskan waters. But again, in a manner that only traditional knowledge can discern, tribal elders note that commercial fishing takes large herrings as well as small ones. They have observed that large herrings show the younger, smaller ones where to spawn. When such "fish wisdom" is decimated by reckless fishermen, spawning patterns can be severely disrupted.

Jeff told me that the Sitka Tribe put forward several proposals to the Alaska Board of Fisheries to reduce the pressure on the annual herring run. All the proposals were rejected, a response that he characterized as "managing the resource for the market, not for conservation." In light of climate change, he felt that it's imperative that marine resources be managed more conservatively. "Something is changing out there [in the ocean] and we need to be more flexible to ensure subsistence harvesters can meet their needs."

Whether herring roe are the proverbial canary in the coal mine signaling imminent catastrophe is not certain. But a signal we must heed is the one from Native people, who live closer to the earth and animals than we do. If the Tlingit are worried, then we should be too. The tear in the medicine woman's eye may not be for her people alone but for all humanity.

Touring Sitka

Sitka neither copes nor manages to just get by. Celebrating its bounty, farmers, and fishermen, Sitkans start businesses, open restaurants that reflect a sense of place, and hold potlucks that bring people together around food and a heartfelt sense of community. They may keep a wary eye on the food barge, salmon runs, and latest indicators of climate change, but they don't accept the bad news stoically; instead, they plan for the future. To get a taste of the breadth of Sitka food life, let's take a condensed and imaginary bus tour:

Leaving from the historic St. Michael's Cathedral (Sitka was founded by Russian fur traders and retains many vestiges of their eighteenth- and nineteenth-century presence, including this Russian Orthodox church), we head over to Beak Restaurant for a quick bite. The restaurant's interior décor immediately tips you off to the origin of its name, which refers to the beak, or mouth, of an octopus. It shares a space in an older but pleasant two-story wood building with KCAW, Sitka's public radio station. Opened in 2017 by Renée Trafton, Beak's menu sparkles with the freshest seafood, local greens, and a scone sundae with vanilla ice cream and chocolate sauce that I'd willingly swim back to Sitka for.

Renée has an outstanding culinary résumé that includes Del Posto of New York City fame as well as some good eateries around Ithaca, New York. She was a philosophy major at Oberlin, so for those who think that students of that discipline have no job prospects, they can eat their hearts out. Renée tells me that philosophy taught her "a sense of agency, and for me, food and cooking were how I achieved that." Local ingredients are at the heart of her preparations. While seafood is easy, fresh vegetables are not, so one of her strategies has been to buy in vegetables from elsewhere that can be grown in Sitka in hopes that farmers will grow more for her than they do now.

Overall, she does pretty well with Alaska ingredients, including reindeer sausage, Delta Junction barley, and locally brewed Baranof Island beer. My tab for a full meal including two beers came to sixty dollars, which I thought was a tad high until I read the fine print: BEAK IS GRATUITY-FREE. That's a little trick she also learned from New York—in this case, NYC's restaurateur-extraordinaire, Danny Meyer. She has fifteen staff who all start at thirteen dollars an hour, the same wage she pays herself. And sixty dollars was my total tab.

Renée "gives back" to the community in ways that don't just mean modest prices, staying open year-round (unusual for a higher-end restaurant in a summer tourist town), and paying fair wages to her employees. She also serves on the board of the Sitka Food Co-op and shares her culinary skills during community food workshops.

Back on the bus, we pass clumps of white-flowered cow parsley that line the roadside and large stands of foxgloves, which grow wild in every untended patch of land. Foxgloves? Botanically known as *Digitalis*, the heart medicine? Salmon and high amounts of omega-3s? I'm starting to wonder if Sitka is naturally heart-healthy. Regardless, our next stop is definitely good for us—it's St. Peter's Fellowship Farm which sits on the back forty of the Episcopal church of the same name. The head gardener of the past eight years is Laura Schmidt, whom we met briefly on the chilly boat ride to Andrea Fraga's Middle Island Garden. This site consists of ten large, meticulously cared for vegetable beds.

The purpose of St. Peter's is quite simple, Laura tells me. "It's to meet the demand for local food." That need was identified at the first health summit, and after some brief discussion with enthusiastic church leaders, St. Peter's garden became a reality. Of course, it took hundreds of hours of volunteer labor to construct the two-thousand-square-foot garden, and by Laura's calculations, another three thousand pounds annually of fish scraps to keep the beds fertilized. Now it's a project of the Sitka Local Foods Network, for whom Laura actually works. The food is sold at the semimonthly farmers' market and the privately controlled but community-oriented Chelan Produce Co., which distributes produce commercially in the Sitka area from April to October.

Like Middle Island Garden, St. Peter's Fellowship Farm and Lori Adams, another small grower down the road a couple of miles from Laura, are growing high-quality vegetables in small spaces for a very appreciative market. The production value per square foot is amazing, but their total revenues assure only very modest returns and part-time livelihoods. In the case of St. Peter's, the small "profit" is used by SLFN to help low-income families start their own gardens.

But the bus driver is waiting for us, tapping his foot impatiently. To make up for some lost time, we've arranged to have a few Sitka foodies come aboard and tell their stories on the way to our last stop. First up is Amelia Mosher, who compares herself to the salmon who return to Sitka every year to spawn. She recently returned to Sitka, her hometown, from a long stint in the Northwest. She's starting a business called Inspired by the Wild, which combines art, natural and local items like seaweed, and beauty products. She is also heading up Sitka's first-ever Mermaid Festival, scheduled for August 2018, where she hopes to highlight the multiple values of underutilized ocean products such as seaweed.

Next up are Jim and Darcy Michener, founders of Alaska Pure Sea Salt Company, which uses seawater right off the coast to make about a dozen different salts for a variety of culinary purposes. It is a going concern with an attractive downtown retail location that markets a beautifully presented product for chefs all over the country. As she put it, learning how to refine salt from the sea in commercial quantities was a challenge to their bodies and domestic life that "probably could have used some marriage counseling." But they got through it and now have a thriving business.

Melissa and Perry, founders and owners of Highliner Coffee Company, tell us that "no coffee is roasted until your order is placed!" As one who frequented the café often during my time in Sitka, I can attest to the coffee's robustness. And even though they didn't mention it, they served the best bagels I've eaten since the last time I was in Brooklyn.

We're back on time just as our bus pulls into the parking lot of the First Presbyterian Church, mentioned earlier as the hoped-for future home of the Sitka Food Co-op. Jasmine Shaw greets us with a warm smile and can't wait to show us around the Kitch. Inside we find a community kitchen that is used for cooking classes and the preparation of commercial processed-food products. Presentations and potlucks take place in the large open hall that's adjacent to the kitchen. Just the night before, she tells us, Sandor Katz, a nationally renowned fermentation expert, gave a lecture that was attended by thirty people. A visiting baker will be conducting a dessert workshop this evening. Two commercial outfits, Simple Pleasures and Captain Juju's, use the kitchen for food prep and processing. Simple Pleasures is a family business with the slogan, "Each berry, handpicked, each jar, hand poured. Artisanal preserves created with love. From our family to yours." As you might guess, they produce a line of jams made from local products, and if you're wondering how they could "handpick" that many berries, well, they have nine children. Captain Juju's is a food truck that sells seafood dishes downtown to tourists and locals.

Jasmine works for the University of Alaska Cooperative Extension Service, which partners with Sitka Conservation Society to operate the Kitch. Like so many projects in this City of the Sea, the Kitch came out of the health summit and was eventually sponsored by SCS in a fashion similar to what they do with Fish to School. As a person who came to Sitka from Long Beach, California, for the first time as an AmeriCorps volunteer, Jasmine can attest to the power of volunteerism.

"You can see the change happen here," Jasmine said. "Sitka's a small town that thinks it's a big town. Come up with a good idea, and before you know it, people will get behind you and pitch in." Even though she's been in town now for a few years, she's still surprised by how quickly things can happen. "So much is going on here that sometimes groups and their events are competing with each other." What's her favorite event? "I'm a hard-core locavore." Jasmine and a small group of colleagues and friends take a whole year to plan for one full week of eating nothing but locally produced, caught, or hunted food—no exceptions. She said that the first year was very hard (she might even have lost a friend or two in the process). "But now it's easier because there are many more local foods options than there used to be."

Looking Toward the Future

The community meeting room at the Sitka Public Library is almost full. Many of the same people I've been interviewing are present, including Laura, Andrea, Keith, Amelia, Jasmine, and Doug. Charles Bingham, SLFN's coordinator, is bringing people to order and preparing to give a PowerPoint presentation to review the past and present state of Sitka's food system. The purpose of the gathering is to prioritize some future action steps.

Attending these kinds of meetings is familiar territory for most of the people in the room, and facilitating them is common ground for the SLFN. Charles, a large man with a bushy Santa Claus beard, reminds the group that SLFN itself came out of the 2008 health summit. Created as a nonprofit organization to promote "the use of locally grown, harvested, and produced foods in Sitka," SLFN was quickly followed by the farmers' market, St. Peter's Fellowship Farm, a garden mentoring program, a community greenhouse, a community food assessment, and food business innovation contest. The last project fostered the development of Gimbal Botanicals, founded by Hope Merritt, that harvests beach asparagus and other sea vegetables, and makes teas, all for sale in Sitka.

After some open discussion, the group was asked to do two things: create a virtual map of Sitka's food system by listing and categorizing all the groups and projects involved with food and related concerns, like health. More than ten organizations and categories (such as government) and thirty-five projects or businesses were identified. The second task was to create a "wish list" of what "we can do to improve our food system." The ideas were fascinating and all over the map. They included creating new food businesses such as grain production, seaweed/kelp farming, and raising chickens and rabbits; reestablishing Farm to School, which had been abandoned by the State of Alaska due to budget cuts; community-based ventures on the order of more composting, excess food distribution to needy families, establishing a community development finance organization to develop and expand food businesses, and perhaps most far-reaching of all—an emergency community food reserve.

The one idea that was perhaps the least concrete but garnered the most discussion was the need for a "backbone organization" that could provide more coordination and leadership. SLFN, SEARHC, and the

SCS have all played those roles, but only on occasion and for select groupings of projects. The consensus was to be proactive about Sitka's food security and to increase the community's organizational capacity to do that. Focused leadership and engaging public policy (i.e., city hall) were now necessary.

Several pages of ideas were copied and photographed. While the next steps were not clearly defined, there was a sense of purpose and perhaps some new energy as people filed out of the room. People had quietly celebrated how evolved Sitka's food system had become over the past ten years—a pride in creating new ventures, maintaining and even strengthening their self-reliance, placing their community's common wealth a little bit ahead of their individual wealth. But the urgency to find a longer-term solution was greater than ever. Whether it was the Blob, the voices of the Tlingit elders, or the barge being two days late (again), those who had brought Sitka's food system this far knew they would have to take it even further.

A community meeting may seem like a small step, but these are the ways that communities network to slowly build their capacity to feed one another, create new economic opportunities, and struggle with the frightening realities of climate change. Projects are initiated, entrepreneurs and leaders are nurtured, and in a less-than-coordinated fashion, the community comes together. In comparison to other places I visited, Sitka appears to be just a little bit ahead of the curve.

CHAPTER 5

Youngstown, Ohio

Youngstown, Ohio has a Rust Belt rap sheet longer than an early Bruce Springsteen song. In a city of sixty-five thousand people that is barely a shell of its former self, it started to go downhill on September 19, 1977, when the Youngstown Sheet and Tube Company announced its closing. Now widely known as Black Monday, that event marked the beginning of the end for the city's and the Mahoning Valley's once booming steel industry.

Other well-paying union jobs would soon fall beneath the bootheel of America's industrial retreat, a decline that disproportionately undid Upper Midwest cities like Youngstown. Just as I began writing this chapter, the Youngstown area added the closing of the Lordstown General Motors Corporation assembly plant to its rap sheet. Only a few miles from Youngstown, the GM facility will lay off its last shift of 1,500 workers in March 2019. Youngstown's newspaper, *The Vindicator*, ran Youngstown Mayor Jamael Tito Brown's statement:

This is just another devastating blow to our local economy. The hard-working men and women of the GM Lordstown plant have been the lifeblood of this community. GM's decision to close the Lordstown plant will have a lasting effect on the entire Mahoning Valley.

The failures of twentieth-century industrial capitalism, which destroyed forty thousand well-paying union jobs from the 1970s through the 1980s, left Youngstown with the unflattering tagline of "the most vanishing city in America." As almost one hundred thousand residents exited the city over recent decades, it was placed on life support through the charity of churches, nonprofit organizations, and government agencies. The Second Harvest Food Bank of the Mahoning Valley (serving three counties around Youngstown) distributed 10.6 million pounds of food in 2017 to its more than 150 food pantry members. More than half of today's residents participate in one or more federal food programs such as SNAP, the Special Supplemental Nutrition Program for Women, Infants, and Children (WIC), or the National School Lunch Program (NSLP). Food insecurity for Ohio overall is 13.7 percent compared to 11.8 percent for the United States, with higher rates generally found in the Mahoning Valley.

Hunger and poverty, direct results of drastically diminished employment prospects, have had other consequences as well. The infant mortality rate for black babies in Mahoning County is 17.7 deaths for 1,000 live births compared to 5.2 percent for white babies. This places Mahoning County eighty-sixth out of Ohio's eighty-eight counties with the highest black infant mortality rates. Similarly, the number of Youngstown's homicides has soared to twenty-eight murders for 2017, which, on a per capita basis, would place it far ahead of Chicago, which had twenty-four homicides for every hundred thousand residents. During just one six-week period in the fall of 2018, nine homicides were reported in Youngstown.

Looking at these numbers forced me more than it did in any of the other *Food Town* cities I visited to question this book's premise that food can make an important difference in the life of a place. Of course, food can make a difference when you're hungry, and like elsewhere, Youngstown has risen to the occasion with its charitable sector and federal assistance programs. But in light of Youngstown's pervasive economic failures, can food really help rebuild this city? As discouraged as I was with Youngstown's underdeveloped food scene, the businesses and organizations I encountered actually reinforced my argument that food can be an engine of revitalization. For instance, the city of Youngstown is one solid food desert. Previous attempts to bring in new supermarkets failed miserably. Yet sixty-five thousand people are consuming roughly half a billion dollars of food every year. That presents a significant market opportunity for the entrepreneurs who can crack the city's food retail and restaurant nut. Second, the energy expended trying to make the city's food system work, by which I mean serve everyone well and lift up the overall quality of life, was significant and occupies a major focus of the region's work.

While it may face a host of obstacles and lack compelling success stories, the Youngstown area (my research took me as well to nearby Warren in Trumbull County) has an abundance of people and projects with the potential to make food a major part of its economic revival. As if to say, "Show me a void, and I'll show you how to fill it!" Youngstown's silent scream is not a death cry but a plea for vigorous, thoughtful, and united action. Though nineteenth- and twentieth-century industrial corporations may have left behind their carcasses in this once proud American heartland city, a mix of "small capitalism," social entrepreneurism, government initiatives, and nonprofit groups, including universities and hospitals, is beginning to reimagine food as a pivotal part of Youngstown's renaissance.

Room to Grow

I'm riding in a car down Youngstown's Fifth Avenue. Liz, a local Unitarian minister's wife and retired technical writer is at the wheel. In the backseat is Karen, a local poet and organizer of Literary Youngstown, a book club whose monthly readings often include food and justice books. Sitting next to her is Hannah, who is studying for her PhD at the University of Chicago by day, bartending by night, and volunteering as a community garden organizer 24-7.

Having just picked Hannah up at the house she shares with several other twenty- and thirtysomethings, we're taking a quick windshield tour of the neighborhood before meeting several other Youngstown foodies for dinner at the Magic Tree, one of the area's very few farm-to-table restaurants. Struggling to be diplomatic, I can't help but express my shock at what looks like some of the most devastated housing stock I've witnessed since a post-Katrina tour of New Orleans's Ninth Ward.

What were once large, architecturally attractive, stand-alone houses are now paint-peeling structures perched precariously on overgrown lots, their windows broken or gone entirely, their interiors darkened and utterly abandoned. On Hannah's block alone, she tells me, fourteen houses, or about two-thirds of all the houses, are completely empty. Only a few blocks away are intact, inhabitable houses that were, in their heyday, mansions occupied by the steel industry's corporate elite. Today, they are going for as little as $80,000 (2016 information).

As Liz snaked her way through half-vacant neighborhoods and around the city's highway system, it became apparent to me that there were few places for people to buy food within Youngstown's city limits. The chatter in the car confirmed my impressions. "There's no food shopping in Youngstown!" "There's a Walmart and a Save-A-Lot out on the edge of town, but nothing in the neighborhoods." "We have corner stores but nothing 'healthy' is sold there." "Poor public transportation makes these places hard to get to." And as one might expect, not only did the city's boundaries separate reasonable food access from almost none, it also contained the region's most economically disadvantaged residents.

As the only passenger in our car who was young and an active bus user, Hannah said that she had to walk twenty minutes from her house to a bus stop, then take a twenty-minute bus ride to reach a shopping destination. Youngstown's status as a food desert had not gone unnoticed by public officials. Less than five years ago, the city government worked with a regional chain to bring three new supermarkets into the city. Due to limited sales and possibly high operating costs, all three shuttered their doors within eighteen months of their openings. Clearly, there was a massive void that the ladies in the car and dozens of other people were trying to fill.

One woman who is trying to close the city's food gap is Melissa Miller. She operates a mid-size livestock farm outside of Youngstown. For years she and other farmers have banded together to sell their products into local school systems as part of a larger farm-to-school initiative. Wanting to expand her markets further, Melissa started selling six pigs a week to Bon Appetit, the food catering company that operates the dining services at Cleveland's Case Western Reserve University. But recognizing the need for local food in Mahoning, she and her fellow farmers formed the Lake to River Food Co-op to expand the market for producers while also increasing options for Youngstown's underserved consumers. Hence, the co-op's membership is now made up of consumers, food processors, and about twenty-five producers.

In Youngstown's North Side neighborhood, the one described above, Lake to River joined forces with the Common Wealth Development Corporation to take over a former bar and restaurant on Elm Street. With financing provided by local, state, and federal agencies, CWDC purchased the building and outfitted the incubator space with an impressive array of commercial food-processing equipment. The building also houses a small co-op retail food outlet and a café that features local food such as Middlefield Original Cheese and Yellow Creek Sausage.

Opened in 2013, the incubator is now used by between twenty-five and thirty small, start-up food processing businesses ranging from salsa and hummus makers to the Shellabella's salad dressing company. On the day I visited the incubator, Maria, who owns and operates the Shellabella's on Main restaurant outside Youngstown, was bottling and taste testing her first batch of Dill Vinaigrette. She was proudly strutting about the café, passing out little paper thimbles full of dressing to patrons, asking them to taste and share their reactions. The feedback was uniformly positive.

Though the economic impact of a small-batch food-processing enterprise like Shellabella's may be small, all the businesses taken together are starting to add up to something. According to Melissa, the incubator and café have met the CWDC's four-year economic development target by creating twenty-eight jobs. Step outside and walk a few blocks north, and you'll see the Saturday farmers' market operating out of the parking lot of the Unitarian Church. If you were there to watch some of the transactions between farmers and consumers, you'd notice special vouchers known as "veggie scrips" being used by some customers. These are issued by Mercy Hospital to its overweight patients with the hope that the additional incentive will encourage them to change their way of eating.

Right now, there is plenty of capacity for business and product growth. Melissa says that the incubator could operate twenty-four hours, seven days a week, but presently is only going at about 40 percent speed. She thinks the co-op ownership model is a good one because it maintains local control and keeps the businesses and members focused on local production, processing, and marketing, which recycles more money in the local economy. Melissa believes that in the long term, food could have a significant impact on the larger economy if restaurants, individual consumers, and businesses, in particular large institutions like regional hospitals and Youngstown University, committed to buying 25 percent of their food from local sources each year. "Our north central Ohio producers," she tells me, "currently have on oversupply of food, and as a potential buyer, the Youngstown market could be a much bigger player." Looking out the window of the café, she gestures toward the street, "and Youngstown's North Side could be the hub for that growth!"

In fact, some of this shift is starting to occur. Because of Lake to River, a food hub has been established as part of a distribution chain that channels goods from farms to institutions. This also includes an e-commerce component that currently provides online local food shopping for forty customers. The Youngstown's food hub is, according to Melissa, one of seven such hubs in the Northeast Ohio region. Based on one study's findings, a shift by buyers and consumers to purchasing 25 percent of their food from local sources would actually create 27,664 jobs in the sixteen-county Northeast Ohio region.

Melissa's hopefulness is tempered by a frustration that the stage is set but only a small number of players show up. The incubator's capacity is nowhere close to being fully used, and the supply of food produced by Northeast Ohio farmers exceeds the current demand. She wonders if cooperation and innovation are simply not part of Youngstown's DNA. After all, this is a former company town where every member of a family had been guaranteed a job for life. Generation after generation never thought that life would be otherwise. Small business start-ups, non-food as well as food, currently have no place to turn to for small amounts of investment capital—$5,000 to $50,000—or technical support. According to Melissa, the state of Ohio and other economic development entities are only focused on supporting science, technology, engineering, and math (STEM) businesses. They have failed to recognize the contribution that food can make to a community's economy.

Similarly, not enough support is coming from Mahoning Valley's institutions. Youngstown University in particular, with almost thirteen thousand students, is not buying locally produced food. Compare them to Case Western Reserve University, where Bon Appetit goes whole hog to buy the whole hog and just about anything else that is grown or raised in northeastern Ohio. From what I could tell, Youngstown University's only contribution to Youngstown's food scene was providing enough student and faculty demand to support the Pressed Coffee Bar and Eatery, the only place I found in Youngstown that made a decent cup of coffee and good cappuccino.

In the meantime, Lake to River acts as a logistical hub for twenty-five producers who bring their product to the Youngstown site, where it is then redistributed to regional buyers. At the neighborhood level, with Lake to River's small retail space and the seasonal farmers' market supported by an abundant supply of special vouchers, residents are given at least a few healthy options.

"Modern Farmers" and Returning Citizens

One of my peculiarities as a child was to watch a Saturday morning TV show called *The Modern Farmer*. In the 1950s, that and moronic cartoons were all you could find at that less-than-prime time. The show featured the newest agricultural technology and farming methods, including ways that you could apply vast quantities of chemicals to thousands of acres, many of which would later be implicated in hundreds of future human and environmental health disasters. The farmers themselves were rugged looking, clean-shaven men with close-cropped haircuts, generally dressed in crisp work shirts and creased overalls. They were topped off with a spanking clean farm hat sporting the logo of one of their agrochemical suppliers.

All of this is to say that none of those images flashing across my black-and-white TV screen resembled Bethany and Corey Maizel, owners and operators of Avant Gardens mushroom farm in Youngstown. Young, long-haired, and tattooed, they wear T-shirts advocating various causes or quirky states of mind that leave you scratching your head as to their meaning. Bethany grew up in rural Western New York and took a job as a produce buyer for Whole Foods in Denver, where she did a lot of high-end organic purchasing and e-deliveries. Since she graduated from Youngstown University, she wanted to move back to the area, partly because housing and land were cheap. They managed to buy a house for $15,000, a direct result of Youngstown's hard times, and decided to get into farming, which is when Bethany's business sense kicked in. They discovered that the small farming communities had become over-crowded with fruits and vegetables producers, so they had to find their own niche: hence, mushrooms.

"It's all about what my mycelium wants," Bethany tells me with a smile. "What makes them happy makes me happy. We especially love our oyster mushrooms. They are the darlings of our farm!" But trying to make it in the Youngstown market didn't prove to be a happy experience. It is still pretty much a hamburger and fries kind of place where mushrooms are found only in cans bearing a Campbell Soup label. She explains how they used a meal and menu app that connects buyers and sellers in a thirty-mile radius. "It flopped in Youngstown, but worked everywhere else. My God! We're freakin' still trying to recover from the steel-plant closings!" But she and her husband are convinced that specialty produce is where it's at, which is why they are embracing what Bethany calls "a quixotic experience."

More entrepreneurs like Bethany and Corey are clearly needed. The imbalance between the supply of locally produced food and the demand for it that Melissa speaks of doesn't apply to the smaller, direct-retail outlets like farmers' markets. Hers are larger growers for whom farmers' markets don't provide an efficient outlet for volume sales. On the first day of the newly constituted Youngstown farmers' market that opened in June, 2018, there weren't enough smaller-scale farmers to meet the demand. They opened at 10:00 a.m. and were sold out by 11:00 a.m.

That year, the market operated only once a month from June to October and was heavily subsidized with a variety of coupons and vouchers that incentivized low-income shoppers to purchase. Adding in the North Side market that is associated with Melissa's organization, Youngstown and the rest of Mahoning County are served by only two farmers' markets. In adjoining Trumbull County, where Warren is the largest city, the story is the same—only two farmers' markets serve a county whose social and economic status rivals that of Youngstown and Mahoning County. According to Cassandra Clevenger, food access coordinator with the Trumbull Neighborhood Partnership (TNP), a nonprofit, anti-poverty organization, their downtown farmers' market performed slightly better during the 2018 season than their inaugural 2017 season. Sales were significantly boosted by the use of double-value vouchers for SNAP as well as a new incentive designed to encourage children to learn more about healthy food they can purchase at the farmers' market.

In the case of both Trumbull and Mahoning Counties, the number and frequency of farmers' markets is considerably below that of surrounding Northeast Ohio counties. Given their lower socioeconomic status, that might not be a surprise. But it's not just a reluctance to buy local produce, it's clearly part and parcel of the larger food-access problems that confront these two places. Crossing the Mahoning River to Youngstown's South Side, I head through what's called the Glenwood Corridor, a section of town that appears at first glance to be green, suburban, and relatively prosperous. I soon realize this is a deception due to the relatively large size of the house lots, which appear large only because there is only one house on them where there used to be two or three. In other words, as the neighborhoods along the corridor depopulated, its houses were abandoned, fell into disrepair, and were eventually torn down. Now this is a largely African American community that may have been relieved of its blight, but not its poverty. The South Side's commercial businesses, bars, and fast-food restaurants are of low quality, and a long drive to a neighboring town is required before one finds a decent supermarket. There are no two ways about it—this is a food desert.

I'm sitting in the office of the Oak Hill Collaborative, a South Side neighborhood action organization, talking with Dionne and Daniel Dowdy, who head up a project called United Returning Citizens. The premise of the group, one I was to find in other forms during my time in Youngstown, was that anybody who could get out of Youngstown in the 1980s and 1990s did. That included Dionne and Daniel, both African Americans who found the city's conditions deteriorating so badly they had to leave. "First came Black Monday, and the steel industry was the first domino to fall," Daniel tells me. "That put my father out of work." Dionne says that was followed by what she called "crack time," the period when the crack cocaine epidemic swept across the country and took an extra big bite out of Youngstown. "This is when families fell apart; children were taking care of children; nobody could buy a home and the city started tearing down the empty ones."

But their homing instincts proved too strong, and their desire to do something positive for the city drew them back. Founding Returning Citizens was a way to encourage others to come home and contribute, while creating a hub for community redevelopment. Each of them made changing the South Side's food environment a priority largely because of their past experiences with farming, gardening, breastfeeding, and preparing healthy food. As Daniel put it, "We need to take a few steps backward to start over again; we need to get our hands in the dirt," referring to his robust efforts to start gardens. To that end, he's managing a three-lot production site across the street from Taft Elementary School, and has a commitment for eight additional lots (there's no lack of vacant land in the South Side) that he would like to cultivate at some point in the future. Daniel's distribution system, which he calls the Community Farm Market, takes several forms, including his own delivery service. While some of the produce comes from his gardens, most of it comes from a wholesale market in Cleveland. One of his distribution sites is 146-unit senior housing complex in downtown Youngstown. Not wanting to limit his work to only food production, Daniel has secured access to a couple thousand feet of potential retail space just outside the neighborhood that he's hoping to convert to a grocery store. "I'm in the busting-a-sweat phase," is how he described the frenzied state of his nonstop, 24-7 community work.

Dionne is equally ambitious though a bit more reserved. She's helping black men who are returning to the community from prison. Her vision is one of numerous black-owned businesses that become a path to self-reliance and serve as an alternative to what she refers to as the "social service dependency industry." She's a dreamer but also a realist, noting that "lots of civic education and reeducation" is necessary to bring the community along. Dionne had a meeting with Youngstown's mayor scheduled to discuss finding a downtown site to sell produce. Interestingly, both Dionne and Daniel spurn traditional nonprofit models, suggesting that these groups are prone to taking advantage of others and that the cycle of getting and spending grants leads to distrust and resentment. "Our goal is to have a farm in the city because we believe in our community and children. And that's how we hope to end this food desert."

Dionne and Daniel point to underlying problems prevalent in Youngstown. But like tangled detritus moving sluggishly beneath an otherwise shimmering surface, tough issues well up from time to time in all the communities I visited for this book. There is energy, there's an emerging cadre of young leaders, there are innovators and risk takers, but there are often entrenched legacies of ill will, racism, and suspicions that threaten to choke the stream before it gains enough force to wash away the old. As Reverend Gayle Catinella, the pastor of St. John's Episcopal Church put it, "Youngstown is twenty-five years behind everywhere else." She cites a history of political corruption that had paralyzed Youngstown, but also a narrative of racism that is palpable. "We have the highest rate of black infant mortality in the country; food deserts in mostly black neighborhoods are worse than elsewhere; black people often can't get mortgages even though housing prices have been as low as eight thousand dollars, and black drivers still get harassed in the suburbs." But like Diane and Dionne, she's taking a stand because she sees no other choice. "I moved here four years ago because I thought I could make a difference. If we don't do something, nothing will get better."

The problems that infect Youngstown are the same ones that prevent nearby Warren's healing. Both cities took a thrashing when Big Steel and the automotive industry left town. Though smaller in population, Warren has a poverty rate even higher than Youngstown's, and its food insecurity levels are comparable. Whereas Youngstown is split pretty evenly between black and white, Warren is 28 percent African American.

Driving from Youngstown to Warren requires an arduous trek along State Highway 422, which Karen Schubert, Youngstown artist and activist, infamously labeled, "the worst fifteen miles in America." You start out passing the blackened dinosaur bones of Youngstown Steel's factories surrounded by hundreds of open acres of empty parking and storage space surrounded in turn by miles of rusting steel mesh fence and barbed wire. The landscape changes though it doesn't improve as the journey drags you by endless commercial strips and shopping centers crammed cheek by jowl with a nauseating array of signs advertising everything except eternal redemption. There are so many intersections and stoplights that my speedometer reading never exceeded thirty miles per hour.

The good news is that unlike Youngstown, Warren has an organization and a person dedicated to community food system work. The Trumbull Neighborhood Partnership (TNP) and its food coordinator, Cassandra Clevenger, have been building community gardens, farmers' markets, and advocating for the development of a supermarket. To pave the way for their work, TNP used a USDA Community Food Projects grant to conduct a community food assessment; the findings and recommendations found their way into the Warren Community Food Security Strategic Plan (2017). Among other things, the comprehensive report calls for improved infrastructure to allow better access to food retail; expanded use of locally grown food in the public schools; and changes in zoning and permitting to allow for more urban agriculture.

Cassandra is hardworking and dedicated, seldom getting discouraged in the face of very tough odds. She's proud of Warren's accomplishments, including a small but budding restaurant, café, and brewpub scene. (The Lime Tree Sandwich Gallery and Modern Methods Brewing Company are definitely worth a stop; the Nova Coffee Co. makes one very superior cappuccino.) Even quirky food connections are hopeful. For instance, Abby Turner of Lucky Penny Farm feeds her goats from Modern Methods spent grain and, in turn, puts them to work munching grass and weeds on vacant city lots. Cassandra is also glad to report a modest increase in participation in their farmers' markets in 2018, due in part to the heavy use of incentives like Double Up Food Bucks SNAP vouchers.

But the externalities that are nearly impossible to control bedevil her. Like everyone I met in the Mahoning Valley, she has few kind words for Ohio state government. To put it mildly, people in this hard-pressed part of Ohio feel neglected, even abandoned by the governor and legislature. Cassandra has made good progress in organizing citizens to attract a grocery store to the neediest neighborhoods, but concern about the city's poor public safety record makes convincing businesses to invest difficult. Summing up her work, which I'd also call her passion, Cassandra says, "We want a grocery store. We want to support better food access with activities that promote dietary behavioral change. We want to put our many vacant lots into food production." She and TNP are riveted on these goals, their methods are sound, and they have a history of success. With a little outside support, they might just succeed.

Perhaps the most positive turn of events for the Mahoning Valley is the emergence of the Healthy Community Partnership (HCP), a major initiative of the Community Foundation of the Mahoning Valley. I'm chewing on a pretty good tuna melt sandwich at the Lime Tree restaurant while chatting with Sarah Lowry, the partnership's director. HCP comprises three health-care foundations that came together to focus on healthy food retail, active transportation, and parks and green space. That could be boiled down to healthy eating and active living, which in most places sound easy enough, but as Sarah makes clear, pose serious challenges in a region consumed by unhealthy food and an addiction to car culture.

Sarah has at least two things going for her: she's very local—raised in the Mahoning Valley and educated at Youngstown University—and well steeped in public policy, having been an aide to US Senator Sherrod Brown of Ohio. Unlike many foundations I've encountered, Sarah's initiative has a long-term funding horizon that will allow at least three years for grantees to show results. Perhaps most important, public policy is not a concept that gives the grantors dyspepsia. They recognize that holding government accountable is a necessary part of social change, and something that foundations must pay attention to. To that end, Sarah explains how community engagement is critical to any worthwhile effort to correct the numerous injustices that have been heaped upon the people of the Mahoning Valley.

Echoing themes I've heard from others, Sarah ticks off the region's problems that the partnership wants to address: "We [organizations in the Mahoning Valley] are prone to 'siloing,' in other words, not collaborating. We also tend to stay with the status quo and avoid risk taking, saying, 'We've always done it this way.' We also don't seek diversity, and as part of that, there is a serious racial divide."

The next day the three of us—Sarah, Cassandra, and I—found ourselves leading a workshop back in Youngstown for about twenty Mahoning Valley stakeholders. The goal for the day was to create a map of initiatives and providers so that attendees could visualize potential collaborations. Once the map was in place, we hoped that people would be willing to find a place where they could connect with others. But before that process began, the participants shared reasons to be both pessimistic and optimistic about the region's food system. The pessimistic flow stayed true to the bad news that everyone had been hearing—high infant mortality and poverty rates—but also underlined a poor history of cooperation characterized by a selfish "what's in it for me" attitude.

But the positive side was far more upbeat than some expected. Participants noted how younger people are returning to Youngstown, attracted by a desire to be a part of a hometown revival as well as the chance to buy an inexpensive house. There was excitement about new businesses opening in downtown Youngstown, including a 1907 historic office building that was renovated as a DoubleTree hotel. The planned opening of The Kitchen Post restaurant with a local food orientation, hip ambience, and cool cocktails was clearly causing a stir. A member of Mayor Brown's staff briefed the group on the Youngstown mayor's Food Access Task Force, which was determined to bring a grocery store to the city. While an undercurrent of skepticism trickled through the group, participants, some of whom were members of the task force, were inclined to give the mayor the benefit of the doubt.

As the stakeholder map began to take shape, it became obvious that there were strong institutions and established organizations committed to similar visions but not yet all working together. Most notable were the health-care organizations, including Mercy Health and the Akron Children's Hospital, which along with county health agencies and nonprofit organizations were represented within the emerging Healthy Community Partnership. Ohio State University's Extension Service was coming to the table, as were groups representing the region's faith communities. Even Youngstown University, with a new course of studies in human ecology, received an honorable mention. While major resources necessary to create transformative change remained elusive, it certainly appeared as if the necessary players and skills were present and accounted for. The only gap was the connective tissue to hold these groups together, a gap that was beginning to close due to HCP and the Youngstown mayor's Food Access Task Force.

The Youngstown story slowly came to an anticlimactic finish at the Draught House in downtown Youngstown, where I sat with Tom Hetrick, a senior staff person for the Youngstown Neighborhood Development Corporation (YNDC). The Draught House is a dive bar whose old brick and polished wood features exude charm if not a faint scent of steelworkers at the end of a long day. Like every other place I visited in Youngstown, it has potential—in this case, potential to be a genuinely enjoyable place to quaff a brew or two with friends, particularly if it offered a more exciting food menu. But the tap selection was good enough, the booths were cozy if not comfortable, and it was quiet, maybe too quiet for a bar at 7:00 p.m. on a Tuesday night.

Tom has a master's degree in city planning and grew up just over the state line in Pennsylvania. He's intensely curious about how communities work, with a soft spot for, as he puts it, "rusty places like Youngstown." He's definitely another one of those committed young people I met, apparently in it for the long haul, having bought a home on the North Side. But another one of his curiosities is food, particularly its relationship to culture, which is at least part of the reason he runs YNDC's food programs.

Though he loves cooking and gardening, Tom is not is an idealistic foodie. When I ask him why YNDC terminated its large urban farm, community garden, and community-supported agriculture projects this year, he tells me they were not reaching the lower-income audiences they were intended to serve. "We had white women showing up from the burbs learning how to make sushi." YNDC tried to run a farmers' market on the South Side, but the community didn't have the density to support it. "None of these projects were able to move the needle on public health."

Tom ran through the same litany of indicators that places Youngstown in the public health toilet. "Our infant mortality rates are at third world levels, and the Robert Wood Johnson [community health] ratings put Mahoning County in the basement." So, he's taking a pragmatic approach. What's the best way to get people to change their diets as rapidly as possible? In Tom's opinion, it's to give them incentives—in this case, various healthy food vouchers—to purchase fruits and vegetables at farmers' markets, one grocery store, and the Lake to River Co-op. "I see lots of pregnant women using our FINI vouchers at the grocery store," he proudly tells me. With a half-a-million-dollar USDA Food Insecurity Nutrition Initiative grant and half a million dollars of matching funds from health-care partners like Mercy Hospital, it's plausible to assume that you can have a bigger impact on people's lives than you can with a garden here and a farmers' market there. Nor is Tom convinced that informational programs are useful, citing a state survey that indicated SNAP participants don't want nutrition and cooking education.

There is an undercurrent of frustration in Tom's analysis. "Youngs-town is so backward!" he says joining the chorus of those who want to see things change but run into a brick wall trying. "People want to coop-erate but can't or don't know how to. A scarcity mentality is prevalent, and when it comes to racial dynamics, well, they're terrible!" So, it's not surprising that he seeks the quickest fix he can, especially when large USDA grants become available and health-care institutions are eager to get on board, and especially when people are suffering as they are in Youngstown.

I remembered something that Sarah Lowry had told me, something that seemed to sum up Youngstown's immediate dilemma, at least when it comes to food, and possibly when it comes to its multitude of other pestering handicaps. There's no one entity that can carry the ball, pro-vide the leadership, or serve as the necessary coordinating hub. There are "boots on the ground" in the form of incredibly well-intentioned people and good projects, but the strands keeping the web intact are weak. There's hope that the mayor can provide some of that glue, but he's young and a social worker by training—not yet, perhaps, the mounted cavalry officer capable of leading the charge of beleaguered troops. When I asked Sarah why YNDC wasn't the entity for Youngstown that they had found in TNP and Cassandra for Warren, she felt they didn't seem to be ready or willing to play that role. So, the search for leadership and a hub are still on.

In the meantime, pragmatism and bilateral partnerships rule. Peo-ple are doing what they can, and what they must. No one is waiting for an economic home run—a reopened steel mill, the appearance of a new dot-com enterprise, or a major league ballpark—to ignite the city's revival. For the foreseeable future, anyway, the groups I met with and the individuals I interviewed are counting on lots of singles coming from the region's farmers, local food entrepreneurs, and the collective action of nonprofits, foundations, faith communities, health-care and

CHAPTER 6

Jacksonville, Florida

"The farm is just blowing up!" "Our food scene is blowing up, man!" "This farmers' market—just look around—it's blowing up!" How many times during my visits to Jacksonville, Florida, did I hear about something related to food or farming detonating? "Blowing up" has at least two definitions, of course, especially in a city known for its major military presence, a 1901 fire that destroyed over two thousand houses, and recent hurricanes (Matthew in 2016, Irma in 2017) that placed many of the city's neighborhoods underwater.

There's the traditional meaning associated with explosives and the resulting decimation of materials, things, and sometimes people. And then there is the hip, slang term for an exciting, nearly out-of-control form of growth, where events are unfolding so rapidly, so unpredictably that they create their own perpetual motion. They breed a swirling form of chaos that is but a precursor to a new, emerging order. When it comes to "Jax's" food system, I learned that both meanings apply.

"It was only a few years ago that people would eat at a local restaurant or have a cup of locally roasted coffee and say, 'That's pretty good for Jacksonville,'" is how Zack Burnett, founder of Bold Bean Coffee

Roasters characterized the beginnings of the city's food scene. "But today they say, 'That's as good as anything I've had in Miami, Atlanta, or New Orleans.'" His appraisal of the qualitative evolution of food and beverages is vigorously affirmed by the eight local food entrepreneurs whose heads nod fast enough to generate a soft breeze across the table. We're gathered in one of Jacksonville's most renowned coffee shops, Southern Roots Filling Station, for a focus group discussion about why Jacksonville's food scene is blowing up, which for these participants does not mean run for cover, but run for exposure.

Unanimously anointing Zack as the "First Foodie" of Jacksonville, his fellow entrepreneurs defer to him for the first response. "Things started to take off around 2010, which fortuitously coincided with the start-up of our coffee business," he says. This was about the time when two or three trends converged to give those sitting around the table the lift they needed. "First, we're giving them good stuff," is how Zack, who is a twenty-five-year Jacksonville resident, describes the dramatic product improvement that was necessary to lure consumers to their goods and services. David Cohen, founder of Manifest Distilling, refers to the time that preceded the current local food scene as a kind of dark ages when an "injustice" was committed against the products that were produced. "This was not the way food should be made!" he said with equal parts outrage and humor.

If you're a snobby foodie, the dark ages metaphor might seem particularly apt when you discover that Jacksonville was an early test site for what was to become the Red Lobster restaurant chain, founded in Lakeland, Florida, in 1968. That creation was followed two decades later by Outback Steakhouse, founded in Tampa, Florida. Nationwide, the two chains have upwards of seven hundred and a thousand restaurants respectively. Since Florida hasn't seen a Maine lobster in its waters for centuries, and Outback is Australian "themed," not owned, these companies project a food fantasy that borrows heavily from Disney World in nearby Orlando.

Mike Schmidt, the founder of Jacksonville's hip Bearded Pig bar-becue restaurant, cut his culinary teeth on food businesses in Boston. He honors the chains' innovation, not so much for a legacy of food quality but for the fact that they were a training ground for many of the region's restaurateurs. "They may not pass today's local food test, but they helped many of us get a start." Just as important to the *real* local food scene's upping its culinary game, however, was the shifting patterns of the region's population. Mike said, "People left Jacksonville and never came back—now they are staying."

Indeed, Jacksonville's shift from a transient US Navy city to one anchored by insurance companies (I heard it referred to on more than one occasion as the "Hartford of the South"), health care institutions, and the financial industry brought people with upscale taste buds and the cash to nurture them. That demand enabled dozens of coffee businesses, cool restaurants, and brewpubs to set sail. Buoyed by the elevation of a food consciousness and associated lifestyle preferences sweeping the nation, Jacksonville's food businesses were ready for business when the consumers arrived and when the Great Recession's dam finally broke.

From the Beach to the Northside

Call me a dog, but my olfactory senses often take over when I encounter a new place. I smell a town before I see it or hear it, and in the case of Jacksonville, September's swampy pallor sits on my tongue like damp earth. Soaking my skin wet before dawn, the humidity swells in uni-son to the sun's ascent until the atmosphere exhales something feral and decomposing. Whether walking on the beach, negotiating a pine tree–lined farm trail, or stepping slowly past the city's office towers, my instincts draw me to the nearest shade or a momentary breeze. Even the gigantic Maxwell House Coffee plant perched at the city's edge provides occasional relief from the jungle odor by enveloping the city in the bit-ter smell of burnt coffee.

As much as cool, dry air is at a premium in Jacksonville, so is beauty. It's a city given over to a functionality that appears locked in a death struggle with Mother Nature for ultimate control of the landscape. Its beaches—"the Beach" is how everyone in Jax refers to their long, thin stretch of paradise—extends southward from the mouth of the St. Johns River. As one of the most walkable, runnable, and dig-your-toes-in-the-sand-able beaches in the country, it's the preferred escape for those hungry for a sea breeze and a place to stretch their legs. But peek out over the rim of your sunglasses, draw a few crude calculations in the sand, and you can imagine the approaching apocalypse. Barely six feet of rising sea—the product of some future perfect storm of high tide, hurricane, and the cataclysmic calving of a faraway iceberg—is all that's necessary to take out billions of dollars of prime real estate.

The St. Johns River and Jacksonville's central business district are spanned by a tangled web of concrete bridges. The river's broad reach and lazy pace drain spongy swaths of southern coastal Florida before its northward-crawling waters meet up with the Atlantic Ocean just east of Jacksonville's downtown. But like a sleeping bear turned grumpy when poked with a stick, the St. Johns's placid waters will rise up in anger as they did during Hurricane Irma, leaving some of the city's tonier neighborhoods drowning beneath its brackish flood.

Through a 1960s consolidation with surrounding Duval County, Jacksonville's big-city ambitions were partially fulfilled when it became the *biggest* city in the United States by dint of land mass. Its population would also grow to the highest, nine hundred thousand, in the Southeast. With all that new land area, the city now spreads gently outward in a series of moderately dense residential neighborhoods punctuated by light commercial developments, railroad tracks whose freight trains stop traffic dead in its tracks for what seems like eternity, hospital complexes, and that ultimate citadel of American "bigness" if not success, sports stadiums. (Jacksonville is home to the NFL Jaguars.) Its medical facilities alone are so dominant that they attract patients from across the South. Their families patronize nearby hotels and restaurants, spawning a robust subindustry I had never heard of—medical tourism.

But the biggest thing about Jacksonville that a visitor will never see is an expansive area north and northwest of the city's Downtown Core. Drive north through the tree-lined Springfield neighborhood, a community with a stunning collection of turn-of-the-century Queen Anne and Victorian-era houses, and you'll quickly pass into the much lower density—and decidedly less affluent—Northside. More rural in appearance than urban or suburban, the Northside radiates outward along extended boulevards that pass vacant lots, run-down and boarded-up housing, churches, gas stations, small shopping centers featuring low-quality retail, and fast-food joints. Though it includes farmland and some working farms, it is, with the exception of a couple of medium-size supermarkets, a food desert.

There's a map of Jacksonville that uses colored dots to locate the number and spatial distribution of the city's racial and ethnic groups. Red dots indicate the location of African Americans, and compared to the rest of Jacksonville, the portion of the map dedicated to the Northside is 95 percent red. It is also an area of high poverty, a fact that is partially disguised by a landscape made verdant by the dense growth of trees, bushes, and grass—the lush products of a steamy, subtropical climate.

Farms, Farmers' Markets, and Their People

Since there is so much water to get past without getting one's feet wet, it seems as though you're always going over a bridge or passing under one. And sometimes you simply find yourself standing beneath a bridge because it's the only place to stay out of the withering Florida sun or a torrential rainstorm. In the case of the Riverside Arts Market (also known as RAM), which is spread out under the sheltering roadways of Interstate 95, the bridge is also the best place to buy locally grown food.

It's Saturday morning in January, and I'm propped up against a concrete highway pillar, talking to Kurt D'Aurizio. Overhead I hear the rumble of trucks and cars motoring their way to Miami and New York. Like many people I would meet over the course of my time in Jacksonville, Kurt is a person of many talents and wearer of many hats. His chef hat is the one that pays the bills, but it's his love of community that ignites the fire in his belly. "I moved here from Atlanta without a job offer when there wasn't much going on," he tells me. "But the food scene started accelerating—it's now a much cooler place."

To prove his point—and demonstrate his love—he enthusiastically ticks off an impressive list of food and beverage establishments whose origins are of recent vintage: "There must be fifteen new brewpubs, including Intuition, Aardwolf, and Hyperion; a dozen coffee shops such as Vagabond, Southern Roots, and Bold Bean; and some really good restaurants, such as Orsay, Black Sheep, and the Floridian [in nearby St. Augustine]."

Acknowledging that Jacksonville is a liberal oasis inside an otherwise conservative and white-bread Duval County, Kurt says that "the chefs and food entrepreneurs are leading the way" to a more vibrant food culture and community. It helps, qualifying his statement with a grin, that "there are people coming here from San Francisco and Portland, including six thousand Amazon employees, who are looking for good food."

Kurt's other hats include his leadership with North Florida's Slow Food First Coast convivium, which, among other events, conducts an annual Tour de Farm that visits eighteen farms in a day. I was to learn later that he was once the head chef of the Sulzbacher Center, the city's largest homeless shelter and rehabilitation center.

Today at the farmers' market, at least sixty vendors and hundreds of customers are swirling around us, including a man being pulled by a Great Dane big enough to saddle. Kurt's wife, Allison, is tending their Flour and Fig bakery and coffee stall where he also fills in when he's not conducting tours for visiting writers. Now a mobile site preparing some of the region's most revered baked goods, Flour and Fig will soon convert to a permanent brick-and-mortar location called 1748 Bakehouse.

At peak season—spring and fall in North Florida—the market is packed with 150 vendors, a number that seems hard to imagine, given how full the site feels on this winter day. Like farmers' markets across the country, the Riverside Arts Market (named by its founder, Dr. Wayne Wood, who wanted to celebrate Jacksonville's arts and culture) has had its existential moments. John Silveira, RAM's manager and a former program manager at the Farm Share Food Bank in Homestead, Florida, tells me that the market had been overrun by "resellers"—produce handlers who were not farmers. His first job as manager was to clean house, so to speak, and to elevate the market to a higher standard of authenticity that demonstrated its commitment to the region's producers. This, of course, paved the way for more farmers to join the market and, more important, to increase the region's number of farmers, particularly young ones. But the change in the market's orientation didn't proceed without resistance from consumers who didn't buy into the local food mantra. "We had to do a lot of customer education," John tells me. "The numbers dropped off after we made the switch, but there's been a resurgence. We still need more demand in order to keep attracting more farmers."

One of those young farmers selling at RAM that morning was Brian Lapinski, who—with his wife, Kristin, a nurse—sustainably operates Down to Earth Farm on Jacksonville's Westside. Brian has what I'd call a practical, anti-romantic attitude toward farming that balances a love of crop production and marketing with a healthy skepticism about the conditions that make it hard to make a living off his five acres. When I asked him why he got into farming—ten years ago, he was a social worker—he laughingly blamed Wendell Berry, who had inspired his interest in agriculture. "I met him once," Brian tells me, "and told him I wanted to farm. He responded by giving me a terrified look!"

Brian's stall was packed with winter greens and flowers, and they moved quickly as his rapport with customers became evident. One lady said, "I love your tomatoes!" to which he responded, "You love my tomatoes, you have to love me!" setting off some giggles that loosened the woman's wallet. But Brian's concerns about RAM and farming in North Florida were decidedly darker. In spite of management's claim that the reseller situation was under control, Brian was frustrated by what he described as vendors who may grow one item but resell ten others. When I asked him if he thought this was a serious problem, he replied, "If you're talking to the angry farmer in front of you, it's a problem."

Brian is vexed by the same challenges that face all young small farmers who have their hearts set on growing food for a community, but wonder why the "community" doesn't show up when the farmer needs them. Down to Earth sells 60 percent of its product at RAM, 30 percent to its on-farm CSA, and the remainder to restaurants. He and Kristin co-market with a bakery called Community Loaves, and they enjoy hosting an Argentinian Pig Roast (an extra-deep roasting pit) as a special event at their farm. "When I started out, everyone wanted a farmers' market in their neighborhood, but North Florida doesn't have enough farmers. I can only think of one new farmer start-up in the last four years." But at the same time, several non-farm retailers offer organic produce in Jacksonville when only a few years ago, no such outlets existed. Brian is glad that RAM and the larger community accept SNAP benefits and have Fresh Access Bucks (Florida's version of increasing the value of SNAP benefits used to buy produce). He's also encouraged that demand for good food is growing, but farms like his that got the local food ball rolling are not necessarily reaping the benefits. A rising tide doesn't lift all ships equally.

One exceptional exception to low farmer growth is Congaree and Penn, a 210-acre rice and fruit farm sixteen miles from downtown Jacksonville but still well within the city's far-flung borders. This lovely property consisting of rice paddies, fruit and olive orchards, and vineyards, is presided over by the perpetually optimistic and glowing thirtysomething couple, Scott and Lindsey Meyer. I remark on their cheery state only because a look around at what they have done in barely five years will leave you wondering how anyone could have done as much they have and still preserve their health, sunny dispositions, and marriage.

Congaree and Penn—an old Louisiana family name—claims to be the only rice farm in Florida (and one of the few in the country) that mills its own rice fresh all year long. It's also home to the largest (and youngest) mayhaw orchard in the world. Mayhaw? Yes, according to Scott, it is the one fruit tree that is native to the Southeastearn United States. The fruit, about the size of a cherry, is incredibly acidic and not suitable for gobbling by the handful. Instead it's best (and most safely) used in jellies and fruit juices. While I wasn't convinced that I should invest in Scott's vision of an ever-expanding mayhaw empire, I would have bought stock in the farm. Its energy and diversity are what you imagine as the future of local farming, with its customer-friendly openness, interesting but not overly exotic product mix, and a marketing reach that's both aggressive and appropriate.

Their stall at RAM was enthusiastically staffed by a woman named Amy, who was the first to use the phrase "It's blowing up!" in reference to the farms' dynamic business model. All the better restaurants and food entrepreneurs I spoke with were talking about (or already) buying rice from Congaree and Penn. (One of my more memorable restaurant meals of the past year was a shrimp and purple grits dish—a variety of Congaree and Penn rice—prepared at the Floridian in St. Augustine.) Their on-farm Farm Table dinners are sold out six months in advance. And after enjoying his meal so much at the Floridian, this writer had to make room in his kitchen cupboard for a ten-pound bag of Purple Rice Grits that he purchased online from Congaree and Penn.

As exciting and promising as Congaree and Penn appears to be, its inland location does not grant it immunity from Florida's sleeping monster—water. Joining a tour group of about twenty people that is led by Scott, I'm as dazzled as anyone by the rice paddies, orchards, and numerous plantings and cleared fields, all of which are easily accessible to Jacksonville's population center. But just to share the whole story, Scott tells us that the place where we are standing was covered in six feet of water following Hurricane Irma. Looking around, I see no rivers, lakes, or other bodies of water. Where did it all come from? I asked Scott. "Out of the ground. There was so much rain that the ground couldn't contain it all," he told me with a shrug.

More Ways to Produce Food

There is the commercial side of Jacksonville's agricultural scene, where farmers struggle to varying degrees to find their niche and earn a living sufficient to support a reasonable middle-class lifestyle. At the other end of the food chain are the buyers, the retailers, and the restaurants who use and celebrate local food—whether it's hyperlocal, sort of local, or in some cases, just loco—to attract customers. Then there is the non- or semicommercial side of food production, which celebrates local food, too, but is motivated by a mix of interests, including community development and public service, food desert amelioration, education, and job training. These enterprises often straddle the fence between nonprofit and for-profit such that I'll call them "profit-fluid." What is clear is that

Jacksonville takes advantage of its year-round growing season to explore every opportunity and technology to grow food for its people.

One of the ways this happens is through what can only be characterized as entrepreneurism in the public interest. In Jacksonville, the best exemplar of this is Nathan Ballentine a.k.a. Man in Overalls. Nathan is a modern-day Johnny Appleseed who hires himself out to homeowners, schools, and anybody who wants help installing or maintaining a vegetable garden. "My mission in life," Nathan tells me, "is to reconnect people with gardening." His father, who grew up in the Springfield neighborhood where Nathan now lives with his family, told him that there used to be several nearby grocery stores, but now there are none. So as Nathan sees it, he wants to teach people to "grow their own groceries."

Take a tour of his front and back yards, and any home gardener will be green with envy. Where grass and typical suburban landscaping once occupied the front yard, collards and sweet potato vines hold forth. Snaking, wood-chip-covered footpaths guide you past a dozen raised beds in his backyard, which are planted in seasonal crops. Fruit trees and other elements of an edible landscape are scattered everywhere. A large area off to the side that has direct street access is given over to a massive compost pile with ingredients delivered by private landscaping companies. But what makes all of this possible isn't just Nathan's horticultural skills; it's his community-organizing orientation that puts those skills to work for people and places that need them. "I'm developing community networks which are flexible and fast ways of delivering information and getting stuff done." One part master gardener and one part community organizer, the Man in Overalls makes an impact far beyond that of your everyday landscaping company.

High-tech agricultural production has become more common everywhere, especially in areas of high population density, where prime farmland is at a premium. In Jacksonville's case, aeroponic, controlled-atmosphere production is being piloted by a small company called Atlantic Beach Urban Farms on the city's Southside. Six-feet-high cylindrical grow towers are producing food inside a greenhouse with a misting system that is directed at the roots of plants such as lettuce. The towers reliably produce food all year round even though the energy costs and the small scale of the operation have prevented Urban Farms from reaching a financial breakeven point. For the time being, grow-tower products have found their way into high-end restaurants, but otherwise are being used for demonstration and education in schools and food banks.

On the opposite end of town, in the city's Northside, Don Lloyd has fashioned an aquaponics system to feed if not the world, then at least the portion that resides in Jacksonville. Called Pura Farms, the operation consists of greenhouses and compact outdoor spaces that house recirculating water tanks where fish are raised and food plants such as lettuce are grown. "We have a social mission," Don tells me. "We're growing in a food desert because the people here need food." The technology works—high-quality food is being produced. And there is certainly a need, since I didn't see a grocery store for miles around. But the enterprise must ultimately make the numbers work. That may be difficult, given that the operation isn't cheap and the lower-income community can't afford high prices for food. In the meantime, Pura and Urban Farms, among other high-tech enterprises, will continue to push the limits of agricultural technology and may one day become a bigger part of their food system.

In a similar vein and also on Jacksonville's Northside is the White Harvest Farms, a fourteen-acre former ash site where currently three acres of land are cultivated in vegetables. The Environmental Protection Agency cleaned up the site so that it is now suitable for food production, and the Natural Resources Conservation Service provided funds to rebuild the soil. The farm is operated by the Clara White Mission, which provides a variety of job training and social services to Jacksonville's most vulnerable populations. Clara White, a former slave, founded the mission in 1904. The White Harvest Farm land was donated by A. L. (Abraham Lincoln) Lewis, Florida's first African American millionaire and founder of the Afro-American Life Insurance Company in 1901. While the farm is a work in progress—plans are under way to add teaching and food-distribution facilities—it is producing sizable amounts of produce for surrounding neighborhoods that have few healthy food options.

To fully appreciate the value of enterprises like these, it helps to know the individual inventor, that single person who lit the spark. That was certainly the case with Tim Armstrong, the mastermind of the business Eat Your Yard Jax, and the nonprofit Berry Good Farms at the North Florida School of Special Education.

Finding Tim's farm on the outskirts of Jacksonville clenches your stomach like reading a few pages from Joseph Conrad's *Heart of Darkness*. The journey begins when you leave the interstate for a state road that turns into a county road that turns into a town road that becomes a forbidden stretch of pockmarked and unsigned dirt road. The progression from light to darkness, dryland to swamp, and noise to silence is palpable. At about the moment you think you're hearing the sound of sizzling insects and chattering monkeys, the forest of long-needled pines opens up into in an unruly Garden of Eden.

Tim Armstrong emerges from behind a curtain of green that is woven from so many different plants, bushes, and trees that you can't distinguish one variety from the other. Between his age, slight build, long hair and beard, North Florida accent, and laid-back demeanor, he reminds me of Tom Petty. (I was to learn later that Tim plays in a bluegrass band.) He gives me just a brief history of himself and the farm—he grew up in the area and was a steelworker until 2008; though not from a farm family, he grew up around gardens and farms, and did some hunting;

the farm we're on is forty acres in size and surrounded by one thousand acres of conservation land. But it's the plants, their names, and their purposes that are Tim's passion.

Edible bamboo and plum trees line the borders, not just "bamboo" or "plum trees" but so many varieties I lose count and my spelling fails me. These are followed by Okinawa spinach, cassava, a couple of moringa trees, pigeon pea, loquat (Japanese plum), rose hips, three varieties of mulberry, and a row of pear trees, just to name a small sampling. As Tim grazes through the planted areas and greenhouses, he's constantly picking off leaves and handing them to me to taste. Politely, I do as he says until about the tenth one, when my palate goes numb. "Goldenrod makes a tea that benefits asthma," he tells me as he pulls out his cell phone for a list of its other curative powers, "It's a diuretic, it's an antioxidant, it's a . . ."

Though his formal training is minimal, Tim is a master horticulturalist whose generous sharing of knowledge is boundless. He seems to have been placed on this earth to convey the miracles of the plant world to the human world. "People are fed up with being sick, and food is a big part of the problem," he says. To that end, Tim pursues his mission of wellness by unlocking the medicinal secrets of plants for a steady stream of customers. They come to his farm, which entertained over six hundred visitors in just one day during a Slow Food First Coast event, and they shop at his stall at the Saturday beach farmers' market where he sells. He extends his knowledge beyond customers by teaching night classes at the University of North Florida, and through thirty videos he has made that are posted on YouTube. And he's even gone global with a presentation at the Slow Food Terra Madre event in Italy.

Though the farm and his teachings would have been enough to secure his legacy, a challenge came to Tim and his wife many years ago that may in retrospect have been both a sign and an opportunity. The eldest of their three sons was born with Down syndrome. When he was older, they enrolled him at the North Florida School of Special Education. The school provides exceptional academic, social, and vocational experiences for 146 people between the ages of six and twenty-two with mild to moderate intellectual disabilities. Tim decided to offer up his services to start a horticultural therapy program for its students, and by the time he was done, the North Florida School had one of the most outstanding displays of edible landscaping and horticultural education I've had the opportunity to witness.

At the school's January 2018 fund-raising banquet, which attracted a veritable who's who of Jacksonville's elite and philanthropists, Tim gave me a tour of the three-acre outdoor garden campus. Fish tanks full of tilapia were circulating their nutrient-laden water into the root zones of vegetable and herb plants. Raised beds were everywhere, fully planted for Florida's winter growing season. He took special pride in showing me the hundred-feet-long rows of blueberries and blackberries that he planted. As he did at his farm, Tim was plucking berries, leaves, and flowers to pass along to me for tasting. The glass of wine I was carrying wasn't exactly an appropriate pairing with Tim's offerings, but it did enable me to swallow a significant amount of raw plant material.

The school is as special as its children and young adults. Distinctive classrooms, a full training kitchen, the gardens, aquaponics and greenhouse facilities, and a food truck are all part of a joyful philosophy that places food at the heart of the educational experience. A focus on occupation drives the program as well. According to Sally Hazelip, the school's executive director, "We want our graduates to be employed one day in meaningful jobs, so they do part-time work on-site." The goal is to create opportunities beyond the kinds of jobs where intellectually disabled people often find themselves, like bagging groceries at a Publix Super Market. Her vision is that the school can help the graduates create rewarding lives for themselves while contributing to the life of their community.

Berry Good Farm, the name the school gave to the growing spaces that Tim created, is very much at the forefront of Sally's vision. Tim was first inspired and later trained by Growing Power's founder, Will Allen, with whom Tim apprenticed for several months in Milwaukee. The tilapia from the two fish tanks find their way into the school's spring fish fry fund-raiser. (About 20 percent of the school's income is self-generated revenue.) A food truck uses food grown in the garden and prepared in the school's culinary program for sale to Jacksonville businesses, food truck courts, churches, and private functions. And from seed to table, the school's young people are cultivating, chopping, learning, selling, and earning their way into Jacksonville's food system.

For Tim Armstrong's part, he has extended the familiar mantra that food is medicine from his remote jungle hideout to the far reaches of Duval County. The yoga moms, with their penchant for right living, are landscaping their properties with the incredible edibles and medicinal marvels that Tim promotes. But at the same time, Dixon, a teenage student at the North Florida School who sat next to me at the fund-raiser beneath a big and beautifully lit tent, told me with a beguiling sweetness how much he loved the school, the gardens, and the food. Tim's skills and commitment have had universal and far-reaching impacts.

Taking Care of Our Own

Profit fluidity, my simplistic term for how organizations and companies prioritize making money as opposed to doing good, may be an understated part of Jacksonville's community life, but the individuals themselves who drive much of the action also move fluidly between sectors. As noted earlier, Kurt D'Aurizio was the head of food service at the Sulzbacher Center and is now co-operating a for-profit restaurant with his wife; Brian Lapinski is a former social worker turned farmer; John Silveira is former food bank staff member now managing a large and multifaceted farmers' market; Tim Armstrong is a former steelworker turned farmer turned horticulture therapist. Far from being chameleons or everyday opportunists, these people and others I met in Jacksonville were guided by internal compasses that generally pointed in the direction of doing the most good for the most people. The job title, the career hat, or the Internal Revenue Service designation of their corporate entities is often only a flag of convenience meant to carry them as far as they need to go to a desired end. Two women who are very active in Jacksonville's food system and embody this dynamic state are Susan King and Ju'Coby Pittman.

The first time I met Susan King, I was standing inside the Atlantic Beach Urban Farms greenhouse surrounded by misting towers that clouded my glasses and made the ink in my notebook run. At that time, she was the business's CEO, promoting the technology for schools while selling some of the lettuce and herbs to high-end restaurants. This job made sense for her since she has a personality so irresistible that I am guessing no one has ever said no to her. But the work, which she eventually left for business reasons, was part of a natural progression for someone who was fervently committed to solving the community's social and economic problems.

Susan, a certified public accountant, joined her head to her heart as a community organizer to lead the Beaches Emergency Assistance Ministry (BEAM), which has a food bank, large vegetable garden, and nutrition programs. "You can't have a community as large as ours [the Beach is a vast area south of downtown] without a food bank," she notes, adding that "there's a tremendous amount of energy for food in this community, and with our vulnerability to hurricanes and the chance that any of our bridges could be knocked out, we always have emergency preparedness on our minds."

BEAM is clearly Susan's crowning achievement, at least so far. A tour of the facility with her and Grace Simendinger, BEAM's development director, revealed a nonprofit organization that put good food and health at the center of its case-management approach. A quarter-acre garden consisting of fifty-five well-maintained raised vegetable beds dominates BEAM's outdoor space. Besides producing six thousand pounds of food for BEAM's food bank each year, the beds provide training and therapy for clients. Each bed is "sponsored" through a $250 annual contribution (the sponsor's name is placed on the bed), thus providing a source of revenue to BEAM. The only downside for the garden—the same one looming over everything in Florida—was that it was wiped out by Hurricane Irma in 2017, even though it's at least a mile from the Atlantic Ocean.

Susan brings her knack for social entrepreneurship to every task. Many innovations adopted by BEAM were gleaned from elsewhere, including a client-choice model that allows the food recipient to select items from different food categories (e.g., produce, dairy) without having someone tell them what they *must* take. Recognizing that her clients face higher-than-average health risks related to diet, Susan instituted a program to increase the donation of fresh produce. Just as important, she brought a full-time dietician on staff to encourage clients to make healthy food choices and to prepare healthy meals. "Wraparound" services were also added to help clients apply for SNAP benefits, rent homes and pay for utilities, and meet other basic needs.

Keeping her nose to the wind and ear to the ground, Susan detected an economic shift taking place in the Beaches' neighborhoods. Real estate prices were rising, forcing people to move so far away that it took three bus connections to get to a food pantry. The people who needed assistance may have been displaced as residents, but they were still present in the Beaches workforce due to the growing number of low-wage restaurant and hotel jobs. In other words, the need for food was growing as was the distance to get help. So Susan invented a program called Live Work, whereby BEAM reaches out to employers that have large numbers of low-paid workers to make them aware of the services. Through aggressive outreach—and by extending their hours to evenings and weekends—BEAM is now able to support the region's working poor, a win-win for employee and employer.

When I last caught up with Susan, she was just starting a new position with We Care Jacksonville, a collaborative designed to improve health care for Jacksonville's indigent families. As she explained the initiative to me, health-care providers in Florida are given immunity from malpractice claims when they are serving indigent patients. Through We Care, services will be expanded from basic treatment to specialties as well such as orthopedics and oncology. They won't be limited to major hospitals either; they will also be available at Duval County's ten free health clinics. (In a rare political moment, Susan made it clear that private initiatives such as these are needed partly because the State of Florida refuses to participate in Medicaid expansion.) Susan has further innovations planned, ones she field-tested at BEAM. Overall, We Care will take a holistic approach to health care for the poor, bringing food pantries and registered dieticians into the free clinics, and supplying healthier food to the hospitals.

Ju'Coby Pittman stood on the stage of the high-ceilinged St. John's Parish Hall, belting out a bluesy version of "Happy Birthday" that made Marilyn Monroe's warbling for President Kennedy sound like that of, well, just another white girl. The former professional blues singer was serenading two people celebrating their special day, along with a hundred others having Friday lunch at Clara's at the Cathedral. As the place for a certain slice of Jacksonville's elite to "be seen," the restaurant also gave lunch-goers a chance to demonstrate their support for the Clara White Mission's culinary training program. And as a special bonus, the food was really good!

Besides being Clara's chanteuse in residence, Ju'Coby is also the CEO of the mission. Its programs focus on job training, housing, and food for Jacksonville's most vulnerable people, especially veterans. The White

Harvest Farms and Market on the city's Northside is its newest program that further extends the mission interests into the predominantly African American neighborhood. Ju'Coby, wearing a long black shawl draped over a black-and-white polka-dot dress that's set off by multiple strands of silver necklaces, is stylish, gregarious, and a proverbial force of nature. But if it looks as though she's calling attention to herself, she's really calling attention to that large segment of the community that is barely treading water, and in some cases, is drowning. Like Clara White before her, Ju'Coby is dedicated to combatting racism and inequality.

"Feeding meals to people can only go so far," she tells me, explaining how the mission has evolved from a traditional charitable model over the last two decades. "Yes, food for today is good, but skills for tomorrow are better. We have to give people tools to be prepared for life." Both the quality and the diversity of the mission's programs are doing that, but Ju'Coby's dynamic presence certainly makes the powerful listen. "I don't take no for an answer. I tell people that if they aren't at the table trying to make a difference, then they're on the menu!" According to Ju'Coby, people return her phone calls, which is part of the reason why Jacksonville's mayor funded a mobile food market that takes fresh, healthy food to the Northside's faith communities. Looking at a map on the Publix Super Market's website, I count twenty stores in Duval County but not a single one in the Northside. That's the injustice that Ju'Coby is fighting.

When issues of racial injustice come up, the engaging impresario turns sullen as she realizes that good programs like hers and the support of the city's white liberals aren't enough. "I stopped at a traffic light the other day," she tells me, "and a man pulls up next to me and yells, 'Motherfucker!' and points his fingers in a shape of a gun at me." Like the hurricanes and rising seas that threaten to one day consign Florida to a watery graveyard, racism, often concealed but now more recently revealed, may yet eat the community from within. She speaks of her thirteen-year-old son, who is telling her that he is hearing more comments about the color of his skin. In a larger vein, Ju'Coby acknowledges that more advocacy is needed to bring the same quality of life to the Northside that is currently enjoyed by the rest of city. "Trust is low among people who live in the Northside," she says. "There have been lots of broken promises regarding new roads and grocery stores since the city consolidated with the county. It's a poor neighborhood that looks like hell, and the elected officials are not delivering."

Later in the summer of 2018, Ju'Coby got her chance to make a bigger difference. She effectively cashed in a portion of her hard-earned social and political capital to receive an appointment by then Governor Rick Scott to fill a vacant seat on the Jacksonville City Council. To underscore her point about elected officials not doing their job, the seat was vacated by a city councilperson who was under federal indictment for fraud and corruption. Ju'Coby had been on the job a total of seventy-four days when she agreed to meet me for a tour of White Harvest Farms. Since it was 94 degrees and very humid, and the farm has yet to build an office, we took most of the "tour" in her air-conditioned car.

Ju'Coby's advocacy and deepening political connections were already starting to pay off. She told me the Northside was beginning to get millions of dollars in new public funding commitments for economic development projects, some of which will expand access to healthy food. But even though she felt good about that progress, she was distressed by what she was learning about the Eighth District that she now represents. "I was shocked by what I heard from some teenagers I met in a middle school. One of them said, 'We can buy guns like tater chips. I need to carry a gun to protect myself and get respect.'" She went on to relate a conversation with a teenage girl who told her, "I can't get help from my mama because she has the same problems I do." If those conversations weren't enough, one of her "get acquainted with the district" tours took her to the city morgue, where she found four dead black teenage boys. Ju'Coby has lived in Jacksonville her whole life and has probably seen it all, but her anguish over this much injustice was clearly evident.

She was down, but not out, saying, "There's a lot more good around here than bad." Though she may have to resort to singing the blues a little more than she'd like, she plans to keep fighting for the quality of life that her council constituents and mission clients deserve. And in the process of doing that, she'll keep food at the center of the fight.

The Northside Food Scene

Just as there are many facets of Jacksonville's food system, there are many facets of the Northside that reveal themselves in unique and often delicious ways. Ju'Coby's remark about "more good" rings true, but making that clear to the rest of Jacksonville is more than just a public relations problem. Cultural barriers, racism, and physical distance reinforce attitudes that promote indifference, wariness, and benign neglect, even from well-intentioned people.

One of the feistiest Jacksonville people I met is Chef Amadeus, an African American culinary wizard who packs more punch in a five-foot-four-inch frame than most people a foot taller. I met him at a focus group in Jacksonville that was organized by Laureen Husband, a county program director for the Florida Department of Health. He told the group that he grew up in Jacksonville, was a private chef, had a specialty spice business, and had been a part of the Seattle food scene, where he said, "food is a religion!" Like others, he shared his concerns about what has been lost: "Everybody used to cook and garden, now they don't. . . . I see kids buying Gatorade—okay, not the worst thing—but they don't know you're supposed to use up calories before you add more." Mike

Swain, a Florida Cooperative Extension agent, agreed with the Chef, "Too many people don't know that a salad is good for you. I've been to too many food pantries that have no fresh produce."

While Chef Amadeus expressed the same disapprobation that everyone did for today's American diet, he reserved a special vitriol for the injustice visited upon the Northside. "It's a 'food swamp,'" he says without suppressing any passion. "There's a fast-food place on every corner, and the healthiest food available is at Subway. The Northside also has the highest rates of illiteracy, crime, and diabetes."

The Chef brought up another injustice that surprised the group. I asked everyone to name their favorite eateries, especially those where they might take out-of-town guests. Their restaurants were largely from the same top-tier lists that by now were becoming familiar to me. None of them, however, were in the Northside. Chef Amadeus pointed out that when local media's white restaurant critics do their reviews and publish their "top ten" lists, they always refer to anything in the Northside as a "hole-in-the-wall." As best as he could discern, these writers had never been to the neighborhood or the restaurants they were writing about.

What ensued was a lively discussion about "hole-in-the-wall" food joints, which led to a spontaneous tutorial from Chef Amadeus. He promptly ticked off a dozen or so names—heavy on barbecue and soul food—that were known to many of group's black members, but few of its white members. Some, he noted, were better than others, but all had historic and cultural roots that anchored the place to the people and the people to the place; in short, they were integral to the community's identity. By the time he was done, everyone was eager to sign up for the Chef Amadeus Magical Mystery Hole-in-the-Wall Tour. And for reasons that were left deliberately vague, the Chef implied that white people would have a more satisfactory experience if they were accompanied by a person of color.

Hole-in-Wall Tour

"I grew up in this neighborhood and came to Holley's to get curly fries during school lunch break." Six months after the focus group, I'm standing on a cracked sidewalk with Chef Amadeus as the first "volunteer" for the hole-in-the-wall tour. He's telling me about the nondescript cinder block building across the street from where we're standing. HOLLEY'S BAR-B-Q the sign says at a busy intersection on Moncrief Avenue, a major thoroughfare that runs east-west through the Northside. The surrounding streets are potholed, curbless, and the neighborhood's mostly single-family homes are in disrepair with piles of accumulated flotsam and jetsam scattered about their yards. As one Yelp review of Holley's said, "The food must be good for so many people to risk their lives to come here." The reviewer still gave it five stars.

When the Chef said, "This is a food desert, but there's always an oasis in the desert," I was skeptical, thinking he was seeing a mirage. The mounting anticipation and scent of barbecue, however, had whetted my appetite, so we sauntered up to the metal-grated ORDER HERE window. I tried the door to get inside, but it was locked. Asking Amadeus where we sit down to eat, he just laughed. "In your car!" No tables, no benches; it's all takeout. The small tarmac apron surrounding the building has live music on Tuesdays and Thursdays. The menu consisted of various combinations and quantities of ribs, chicken, oxtails, and curly fries. I ordered the smallest portion available—three ribs, curly fries, and an orange soda (no alcohol is served at Holley's)—only to take half of it home in a sodden clamshell container.

Before we could make our way to my car to dig in, a large black Escalade pulled up, driven by Wendy, Holley's proprietress. Of course, Chef Amadeus knew her well, and during my time with him, I discovered that everyone in the Northside knows the Chef. I asked her if it's true that this is where curly fries were invented. "My dad's brother, Leroy, made the machine that curled the fries," she said. The Chef wanted to know if she still had it. "I could dig it up. My dad could have had a patent on it, but he couldn't read nor write, so he got bamboozled." Wanting to get Wendy to talk a little more about her business, he prodded her with, "When they write a food blog, they never write about this part of town." "You know why!" Wendy responded in the eye-rolling way some black folks have of saying "racism!" without actually saying it. "I get my recognition from the stars who perform in Jacksonville—the musicians, rappers, comedians. After the show, what food do they want? Not that fancy stuff downtown. They want mine!" After I eat Holley's ribs—meaty, tender, covered in a sauce you'd crawl for—I can honestly say I want her food, too, but probably just once a year.

"What black culture and food are all about is that everyone comes to a place where everybody knows everybody." Thus spoke Amadeus, though I also hear the *Cheers* theme song playing in my head. As I walk into Celestia's Coastal Cuisine, an African American seafood restaurant several miles from Holley's but still in the sprawling Northside, I can't imagine a team of academic sociologists saying it any better than Amadeus. The place is hopping, a buxom lady blues singer is killing one heartbreak ballad after another, and Varon Mobley and his wife, the restaurant's namesake, Celestia, are cooking and serving shrimp, crab, and oxtail dumplings to a laughing crowd of fifty or more. It takes me about three seconds to realize I'm the only white person in the place, but I feel un-self-conscious, even loved, and like, well, everyone knows my name.

While Holley's is rough-and-tumble—located in a part of town where, I'm told, "when you hit a red light, mister, you don't stop!"— Celestia's neighborhood is decidedly middle-class—formerly rural and white, now 80 percent black and mostly suburban. And as I was to learn from Celestia herself, it's far more sacred than secular. Her culinary roots are long and deep in Jacksonville, including culinary training at Florida

State College in Jacksonville, and a long stint at Soul Food Bistro, a local institution associated with the Potter's House Christian Fellowship. The Soul Food Bistro has brought African American cuisine to both the east and west sides of Jacksonville, making it a cultural bridge of sorts. But most important, it infuses its menus and staff with an open, heartfelt, and nonjudgmental Christian spirit.

"We opened Celestia's eighteen months ago, after consultation and prayers with our pastor," Celestia tells me. As such, this restaurant is "an old, new place"—an extension of her faith and the Potter's House church. When I ask why she chose food as a career and as a way to express her faith, she says, "I love to make people happy; I associate crabs and good food with family and being together." When I ask for a favorite line of Scripture, she doesn't pause: "All things work together for the good to those who love God."

On my better days, I would also consider myself a believer, but I still want to find proof in the food and the chatter. Celestia honored me with a heaping platter of whole crabs and shrimp, which after not finishing my "child size" portion of ribs at Holley's, put me to the test. After seeing me struggle with cracking open the crab shells, a nice lady by the name of Nikki Nixon offered to help. She was dressed to the nines—bejeweled and hair styled for a night on the town—but that didn't stop her from grabbing the sides of each of my three crabs with her perfectly manicured hands and breaking them cleanly in half, revealing a treasure trove of meat. We both had a good laugh!

Southern Roots

The Southern Roots café group discussion was winding down. Besides the coffee roaster, baker, distiller, aquaponics promoter, and restaurateur, I had heard from Shai Tzabari of a fermenting company called Olive My Pickle, Brentley Stead from a honey purveyor called Bee

Friends Farm, and Meghan Fiveash of a three-store independent natural grocer called Native Sun. Each story was filled with entrepreneurial risk taking, growth, success, a fair amount of luck, and a singular dedication to quality. Collectively, the businesses at the table had created about two hundred jobs over the past ten years, and were at the heart of Jacksonville's food revival. Notably, they helped each other and operated under the assumption that if any one of them failed, it would be as if all of them had failed. A strong ethic of mutual support informed their work. Tacitly, they subscribed to the lengthy Southern Roots mission statement and principles prominently displayed on a nearby wall, prizing integrity, sustainability, quality, people, and respect.

What struck me most about the differences between the food entrepreneurs who were white, and the Northside restaurateurs who were black was that the entrepreneurs do not conduct any significant amount of business in the Northside, while the Northside entrepreneurs probably wouldn't be caught dead publicly articulating a comprehensive list of principles like those at Southern Roots. Does that mean the two camps are so far apart that the twain shall never meet? I don't think so. Certainly, they each operate in their own cultural spheres, don't seem to need each other, and aren't the worse for wear for not intentionally finding common ground.

Whereas the black community has forged a bulwark of armor to ward off the slings and arrows of hundreds of years of oppression, the white food community has carried the cross of sustainability, localism, and connectivity against the outrageous fortunes of an industrialized and indifferent food system. Somehow, I detect the scent of a potential alliance in Jacksonville. Somehow, if the white folks could venture into the Northside, enjoy the conviviality of breaking bread together, and reflect more deeply on racial injustice; somehow, if black folks closely considered environmental implications of Scripture, such as humankind's stewardship over God's creations, and the healing powers of true forgiveness genuinely sought, then maybe food could emerge as a force powerful enough to create a robust economy with a much larger and more diverse cast of winners. Such a partnership, forged in a common kitchen of goodwill and cultural respect, might even stem the rising tide of racial injustice and climate change. Call it a faith in food and its inherent power to heal.

Jacksonville Is Blowing Up

It has been alleged that the farther north you go in Florida, the farther South you go. If the measures are racial segregation, poverty, food deserts, poor dietary health, and generally conservative politics, North Florida and Duval County are more akin to the Old South, while Jacksonville proper—the downtown, its nearby neighborhoods including the Beach—behave more like the New South. Broad characterizations like these are fraught with peril, but if you look at Jacksonville through the proverbial food lens, contradictions do stand out.

"Food can destroy a community, or it can make a community prosper," is how Laureen Husband puts it. Through her work with Florida Department of Health as the former Director of Healthy Jacksonville, Laureen has seen the gross disparities that keep so many people hungry and sick, but she has also seen the promise of a robust local food economy meeting everyone's needs. Through her organizing efforts, she brought the Duval County Food Policy Council together, and during her tenure as the health department's representative, the council changed school policies to promote healthier food, developed school gardens, changed purchasing regulations to secure more locally produced food, and made farmers' markets accessible to lower-income and SNAP consumers. One of the council's more striking achievements was to bring a measure of coordination to the chaotic process of fund-raising, which is often an "every man for himself" experience. The food policy council was able to effectively match grant opportunities to the most qualified applicants.

Partly because Laureen left Duval County for another health department assignment, the Duval County Food Policy Council languished until it folded a couple of years ago. "We still have a hunger to connect," she said, "because there is so much good food work going on, but without something like the FPC, the work is disjointed." All those I talked to in Jacksonville expressed a similar sentiment. Susan King is moving forward with a bold health-care collaboration that promises to bring much-needed medical services to the city's poor. Mike Swain from Florida Cooperative Extension and Ju'Coby Pittman are trying to build collaborations among food pantries, farmers, and nutrition educators. "Agriculture and health are obvious partners, but they need to improve their coordination," Mike said.

The City of Jacksonville has only recently begun to develop a significant food portfolio. Ju'Coby Pittman's appointment to the city council should help leverage more public resources, a fact made evident by the mayor's recent commitment to address the food desert problem. Along with an activist and empowered citizenry, especially its food system stakeholders, city hall must play a bigger role to address not only immediate food and health problems but its social and environmental challenges, as well—all of which requires bold leadership.

The food sector in Jacksonville is "blowing up." To echo Zack Burnett from Bold Bean Coffee Roasters, Jacksonville's food scene is good not only for Jacksonville but for everyone who participates in it. While the excitement and fun associated with that explosive energy should be continually enjoyed and nourished, it does indeed need to reach everyone. As I discovered, there are cultural differences in the city's food worlds that can serve as a silent wall between the privileged and those who are victims of historical oppression. But those differences can also

CHAPTER 7
Portland, Maine

As a college student in Maine in the late 1960s, I was often advised in loco parentis by the school not to go to Portland. Such admonitions, of course, only serve to pique a twenty-year-old male, and the more often these warnings are heard, the sooner his desire becomes a palpable itch that must be scratched. The Down East seaport city of that era was indeed a boozy and brawling place where eating lobster in the rough was often accompanied by some rough treatment. Should we succumb to Portland's temptations (and we did), we were told to travel in a group that should include the largest football player available. And as Maine's only municipal jurisdiction that actually qualified as a city by dint of density and population, it was the closest "social problems laboratory" for a sociology major like myself.

When it came to food, the iconic lobster was it. Having ascended early into the small pantheon of universally desirable American edibles, those wriggly red guys were an easy choice for any culinary parvenu wanting to display a little flash and class in the kitchen. As one of nature's most delectable and nearly ready-to-eat foods, lobsters were hard for even the most incompetent cook to screw up—provided, of course, that boiling an animal alive did not overly offend your sensibilities. Beyond that, Maine and its biggest city, Portland, had little to offer the discerning eater beyond the ubiquitous spuds and clams. As John Naylor, owner of the Rosemont Market & Bakery chain would tell me, Portland's most popular piece of kitchen equipment was the deep fryer. When the grease-laden smoke of a hundred or so of these belchers would blend with the briny stench of low tide, the Portland waterfront sank into a putrid haze that rivaled the worst days of freeway-enveloped LA.

But, my oh my, what a difference a few decades can make! As a city that was experiencing a steep population decline in the 1970s, Portland is now growing as much as its peninsular land base will permit, and now stands at over sixty-seven thousand residents. A waterfront that was once home to vegetable canneries and shipping terminals for Kennebec potatoes (sent to Idaho, of all places) has been converted to condominium developments where individual units go for at least $500,000, and to marinas providing safe harbor for yachts. As one of the Northeast's best deepwater ports, Portland was a great shipping center that, among other uses, served as Montreal's winter port because the water didn't freeze. But today's gazer upon the seas will not see a tangle of masts, yard-arms, and rigging. Instead, he will take in, over the course of the warm weather season, as many as 160 cruise ships disgorging thousands of tourists hungry for the taste and look of an old New England seaport that is a reasonable facsimile of its former self, minus switchblades and deep fryers, of course.

While many tourists will no doubt be thinking "Lobster!" they will have some three hundred restaurants to choose from that fly the flags of all the generally recognized cuisines as well as the more exotic ones from Ethiopian to Vietnamese to Maine. In the latter category, they can select from everyday, pricey-local like Street and Co., which does a phenomenal job with nearby beets, kale, and a catch of the day (like halibut), right off the fishing boats. If that's not authentic enough, seekers of the uniquely Maine can go to the militantly local restaurant Vinland, whose chef would sooner fall on his ulu knife than serve something that was not grown, raised, or caught within fifty miles of Portland. It has a mission statement and list of principles that run for several pages on its website where it also claims to be, "the first restaurant in the United States to serve 100 percent local, organic food." It was for reasons of quantity, diversity, and quality that the *New York Times* singled out Portland's restaurant scene as one of the best for a small city in the nation.

Portland's topography invites comparisons with San Francisco. A steep descent from a summit dominated by the Maine Medical Center, Portland's largest employer, to the water's edge takes you through a well-preserved downtown. Nineteenth-century brick buildings and cobblestone streets that meander in ways that defy intentional design become more charming the further that American cities distance themselves from their past. Shops and sidewalk cafés (warm weather only, thank you!) cater to tourists, of course, but there is nothing that slaps you in the face as a tourist trap or bourgeois or simply overdone. It's a city of real people who are creating an identity and a style that are unique to them and their place. Some collective civic consciousness had the foresight to recognize that Portland's historic bones were solid and should not only be preserved but reinvented in a fashion that could admirably serve the visitor, the native, and newcomers seeking native status. And, of course, food has played no small role in the city's current reincarnation. Even a standard bit of street fare like the Mark's Hotdogs dog cart on Market Street gives off its own Portland vibe—seagulls are scooping up stray bun crumbs rather than pigeons.

There's another tale to be told about the city and its food scene, one that will never be known by the cruise liner crowd who have eight hours to "experience" Portland. I discovered it early one morning, standing in line for breakfast at the Preble Street Resource Center with the city's poor and homeless who were shaking off Maine's November chill. The place was packed with haggard-looking folks for whom a good night's sleep would be a cherished gift. My plastic tray was filled by local church volunteers with two fried eggs, sunny-side up, a couple of slices of white toast, and some aromatic beans. (I didn't ask if any of this was organic or local.) A spoon and fork were the only utensils available. When I asked, "Where are the knives?" I answered myself with, "No knives. Oh, I get it!"

Clutching my tray firmly to avoid a collision with one of the 150 or so guests, I huddled in the quietest corner available with Mark Swann and Donna Yellen, Preble Street's executive and deputy directors respectively. We're surrounded by people who are hungry, cold, homeless, disheveled, and many of whom are struggling with drug and alcohol addictions. I will confess that they are not people with whom I would want to spend most of my day. Yet Mark and Donna handle a scene that teeters on the brink of chaos with the aplomb of two gentle sheepherders. They are composed, highly trained social workers who know how to work with people under the kind of stress that most of us can't even imagine; they are compassionate servants providing a host of services to Portland's most vulnerable, yet they are politically savvy. They empower their clients to fight for their own needs while mobilizing statewide political and funding support to expand protection and services for those clients. Their attention is riveted by dozens of short-term crises popping like firecrackers around them, but they never forget the complex socioeconomic and political problems that cause these crises. In short, they are two people I would want to have on call if my life were about to become seriously unraveled.

I learn that I'm witnessing the tip of an iceberg that has moved with glacial slowness across Maine's landscape for many decades. Between Preble Street's several shelter, meal, and pantry programs, it's serving

1,100 meals a day that are frankly a lure as much as they are the only source of nourishment for a large number of Portlanders. "Food is the hook we use to get people to help themselves." Donna tells me, "We sit down with people to eat and to engage." By that, she means that the need for food is what brings them to Preble Street, but the literal milk of human kindness is what opens a window into a world of other needs that arise from a long-term interplay of economic, social, and political forces. I'm reminded by Mark that, like hunger, homelessness barely existed in the 1970s. Cheap rents throughout Portland, partially a function of its depressed economic state, made finding housing a fairly easy affair. However, renters were exploited by ruthless landlords, which provoked a series of housing rights struggles. But as cities like Portland recovered and became trendy, housing availability declined and prices went up.

While those events explain the homeless crisis, they don't tell us why so many Mainers became poor. To sleuth back further into the state's history, I turned to another Mark: Mark Lapping, Distinguished University Professor at the University of Southern Maine Muskie School of Public Service. Maine was a natural resource state, he tells me, that harvested timber to build ships, and later to make pulp for paper; its rivers powered the textile mills that spun wool and cotton into fabrics, and whose waters would serve as receptacles for factory effluents. Though America's deindustrialization more or less began in the late 1960s, those industries would first move to the South and then offshore or simply disappear altogether. To put it harshly, Maine would become one of the big losers in the race to the bottom. This left behind a large unemployed blue-collar workforce and wretchedly polluted rivers. With no work, residents moved to the state's small number of cities like Portland. But what they would find in this city by the bay was an emerging trendiness characterized by the popularity of places like L.L.Bean just down east a piece in Freeport, a growing restaurant scene, and a gradual influx of young people stalking the eternal "hip" by way of the latest craft brewery, cidery, and distillery. Portland had burnished its rich seafaring past to make it, as Lapping put it, "a little gem, but a reflection of the American paradox—wealth and abundance side by side with scarcity."

Local Food

I'm sitting at water's edge with my brother, Eric, looking out over Casco Bay from the comfort of the Flatbread Company restaurant. He's lived in Maine his entire adult life, having actualized my fantasy of clearing your own land, building your own house, and starting a successful home-based business. I would have done the same if I knew which end of the hammer to hold. He tells me that one of his enjoyments in life is to go for a long walk on a cold winter's day, then warm up by the wood-fired pizza ovens in Flatbread. Only a Mainer could take such delight from turning pain into pleasure!

We decide to share—something we never did very well as children—a large salad whose greens are local and organic. Deciding to split a large pizza after arguing a bit over the toppings—homemade Maine maple syrup flavored fennel sausage, their own tomato sauce, local herbs, and Sunset Acres goat cheese—we grab a couple of beers brewed according to the menu, .6 mile away. We'd ordered a large pizza assuming that Eric would take the leftover slices home, but it's so good, we find ourselves squabbling like twelve-year-olds over the last slice.

That evening, my "local" eating experience was decidedly different but no less authentic than the one at Flatbread, or the evening before at Street and Co. Just one pier down from Flatbread, and this time on my own, I find my way onto a dimly lit wharf, circle behind a nondescript one-story building, and almost fall into the drink at the dock's unrailed edge before finding the entrance to J's Oyster. Rather than the tweedy,

L.L.Bean-dressed crowd from Street, or the untucked and bearded hipsters from Flatbread, I stumble into a proletarian bar of flannel shirts and fisherman caps where a hollow-cheeked waitress greets me with a genuine, "Hi, hon!" It's crowded, and the tables are assembled cheek by jowl, perhaps to simulate conditions in the nearby lobster tank, where the divine crustaceans awaited their final solution. The experience is *very* local, way before local was "local." And the raw oysters were sweet and plump with just the right amount of brine, while the lobster was, well, to die for.

One could forever wax enthusiastic about Portland's food scene—its too-numerous-to-count brewpubs, oyster bars, and coffee shops. Different data sets from various sources even make the claim that Portland has more restaurants per capita than any other city in America, including San Francisco. Food miscellanea and trivia abound: former Portland Mayor Michael Brennan told me in 2014 that *his city* was selected by *Travel + Leisure* magazine as the number six best city in the country to get ice cream, and I have never known a mayor to lie about ice cream.

While Portland's infectious food scene has a devoted set of followers, the faithful who subscribe to the tenets of "locally grown" may, in fact, constitute a religion. If that is so, then Maine's own Helen and Scott Nearing would be its messiahs if not its creators. Their book *Living the Good Life* is about as close to a bible as localism will ever get, published as it was in 1952, shortly after the Nearings started their legendary homestead in coastal Maine. Living almost three weeks beyond his hundredth birthday—a testament no doubt to his "simple living" ethos and vegetarianism—Scott Nearing was also a radical economist and peace activist. His spirit of self-reliance and a back-to-the-land individualism live on in the thousands of young and not-so-young Mainers who adopted lifestyles and values in alignment with those of the Nearing's. (With the fantasy of living that dream myself, I came perilously close to buying a run-down old Maine farmstead right out of college, with no amenities, until I realized I'd have to give up cold beer.) Today's renaissance in small-scale agriculture and Maine's first-in-the-nation food sovereignty law, which streamlines regulations to facilitate the flow of locally produced food to the state's food outlets, can trace their lineage back to Helen and Scott Nearing. And you can see their legacy reflected in the faces of the thirty or so farmers at the twice-weekly Portland farmers' market.

One of their descendants, so to speak, is John Naylor, founder and owner of the Rosemont Market & Bakery. John opened the first of what are now six grocery stores (four are in Portland) in 2006 by taking over the former Portland Green Grocer. In his early sixties, John is what I would characterize as a pragmatic hippie entrepreneur who brings a tough work ethic to bear on a clear-eyed vision for his community's food future. He's the kind of guy who displays his enthusiasm for his business and products by rhythmically pounding his fist on the table to punctuate his every point. If his argument doesn't persuade you, you will inevitably fall into step with his drumbeat.

Visit his store on Commercial Street, which, like all the others, has a noticeable European flair—even if you're not sure what a European flair looks like. A great selection of wines, local craft beers, cheeses—imported, domestic, and local—a beautiful butcher shop, bins of local fruit and veg, homemade and homegrown baked goods, and a lovely prepared-food section are all tucked snugly into a couple of thousand square feet. It's cozy, cute, woody, and without a doubt, the shopping experience is satisfying and stress-free. By no means does every product in the store come from Maine sources, but it has a "Maine first" policy that gives preference to those products when available. And John works harder than most people I've met in the retail side of the food business to make local food available. "Maine had a great peach crop last year [2017]," he tells me, "so we didn't buy them from South Carolina and Georgia. We push the envelope by doing something like featuring spring parsnips (Maine grown), which are incredibly sweet when they've been held over in the ground all winter long."

Part of John's success comes from combining his management acumen with his local-first ideal. In response to the growing demand from his customers for more local food, he analyzed his various business systems, including purchasing, billing, payments, labeling, logistics, warehousing, and transportation. He found that with improved integration of these systems, more Maine farmers (150 farms now sell to Rosemont) could be reached more efficiently to bring a greater diversity of products to his market. For instance, listing all their active farmers and contact information, Rosemont could map out the farmers' product lists, locations, estimated quantities, and varieties. This would enable all six stores to match current demand to supply as well as project future supply. Through in-store information and labeling, for instance, John will tell his customers more about an item's origins and production methods than perhaps they want to know. But that's okay, since, as John puts it, "We want to feed their curiosity, not just their hunger."

If the religion of localism has a set of sacraments, perhaps handed down from on high, they would prescribe ways that a buyer should treat her producers, as in "Thou shall be transparent!" "Transparency," according to John, "is what it's all about. They know what I'm doing and I know what they are doing." As a sign of respect, John pays his farmers (and other vendors) within seven days, something that's uncommon in the world of food retailing. And for Rosemont, doing things the local way doesn't stop with its food vendors, it also applies to the plumbers, electricians, banks, insurers, and other service providers that a grocery store needs to stay afloat. This is how a business connects to a market that also happens to be a community. It's also how Rosemont built its business from one store, $200,000 in first-year sales, and five employees to six stores, $10 million in annual sales, and almost a hundred employees today.

Local is a powerful economic engine that connects many community dots, but it's also one that is fueled by a special kind of soulfulness. At the risk of straining the religious metaphor, I was struck by the way John described one of his vendors, Caldwell Family Farm, a thousand-acre operation located in Turner, Maine. Over five hundred beef cattle graze pastures that have been certified by the Maine Organic Farmers and Gardeners Association. Caldwell is also one of only five US farms to have earned a Step 5+ rating from the Global Animal Partnership. As John describes the life of their cows, they spend their days munching some of the healthiest grass in New England while gazing out at a million-dollar view of New Hampshire's White Mountains. "The only bad day of their life is the last day," he tells me. "The farm's slaughterhouse is well lit, and the walls are painted with bright colors. The path to the slaughter-house is lined with flowers to set the cows at ease. They never go alone or one at a time, but they go with mates. The farmer wants his cows to feel like they are walking into heaven."

Cultivating Community

The Rosemont Market & Bakery grocery stores are not for everyone. Portland's one Whole Foods Market, where I sipped a cappuccino late one afternoon, probably does as much business in a month as John Naylor's six stores do in a year. Conventional chain supermarkets spot Portland's perimeter and nearby suburbs as well, giving consumers plenty of options, none of which, however, are as committed to local sourcing as Rosemont. But the fact that a small city and its surrounding metro area can support so much food-shopping diversity, to say nothing of the vital small farm scene within a fifty-mile radius, speaks volumes about Portland. Still, diverse shopping opportunities don't necessarily mean that a place's food system responds fully to the place's diverse communities. That's where the eighteen-year-old nonprofit organization Cultivating Community comes in.

I'm sitting with the organization's executive director, Craig Lapine, in the kind of unkempt office that takes me back to my former non-profit days. Gardening implements compete with stacks of reports and brochures for space in untidy corners where you'll also find expressive photos of gardeners and beautiful images of vegetables. Though not presented in an organized, gallery-like manner, the photos scattered about the office tell a multicultural, multiracial, and multigenerational story about who gardens in Portland. Young people, elderly people, and people from African nations where famine and civil war still reign are smiling, leaning on hoes, and bringing plants to life in Maine's not always forgiving soil.

One can only trust that the staff will find those lettuce seed packets from among the clutter before next spring. But as its office seems to be saying, Cultivating Community has so much going on that its activities threaten to burst the seams of its mission statement. Apologetically, Craig shares its somewhat uninspiring words: "to improve access to healthy, local food and teach and empower people to produce food." But he becomes more assertive when he adds, "We've chosen to express it differently by emphasizing farmer training, youth development and leadership, and food justice."

Like many organizations of a similar ilk, Cultivating Community has gone beyond the traditional role of managing community gardens and showing the horticultural flag in oftentimes plantless urban environments. Today, it is embracing an ethic that puts the "community" ahead of the "cultivating" as it acknowledges the city's systemic failures. Like Mark and Donna at Preble Street, Craig sees food as a means to attack structural inequities that lead to poverty, hunger, and homelessness. "Food is a starting point, a way to bring people together, and a bridge to a more systemic form of thinking about the environment and health."

Craig will be the first to admit that his organization has benefited from the tidal wave of interest in local food and farming. "In 2002, right after we started, it was hard to make an argument that food was an environmental or health issue, particularly with funders." But suddenly things began to shift. Cultivating Community was able to increase the number of Portland's community garden plots from 140 to 500. "Prior to that," he said, "plots were so scarce that someone had to die before a new person could get one." By 2007, college kids from Maine's elite liberal arts colleges were beating down Cultivating Community's doors for internships at such a rate they literally had to lock the office doors. At the same time, the city's restaurant resurgence was turning its chefs into hotshots who were churning out gourmet feasts beneath candlelit tents on nearby farms.

But another wave that started as a trickle in the early 1990s began to crest shortly after the dawn of the twenty-first century. In 1990, Portland was one of the whitest cities in America, with only 3 percent of its population being African American, Hispanic, or Asian. According to the 2010 census, white people made up only 84.6 percent of the population, and the percentage of African Americans had increased to 7 percent. A good part of the change was due to the influx of various immigrant and refugee groups, especially from regions overwhelmed by civil strife, such as Africa and the Middle East. Today, twenty-seven languages are spoken in Portland's public schools, and organizations like Cultivating Community must translate their printed material into several different languages.

These demographic changes meant that Cultivating Community had to recalibrate the way it did business. The expanded number of community garden plots gave them the opportunity to ensure that they served more people in need. Craig estimates that 25 percent are now occupied by low-income families. Internally, they realized that their own staff, including lots of smart, well-intentioned college interns, did not reflect the community they were serving. Thereafter, more internships started going to Portland high school students, and staff positions were going to more people of color. Programmatically, they started more food-production training programs for youth and "New Americans," the term they used to describe recently arrived refugees and immigrants. The food produced in those training programs would be distributed through free and low-cost CSA shares to places like Franklin Towers, the city's low-income senior housing complex, and to lower-income neighborhoods via a mobile farmers' market that's called the Good Food Bus. One example is a New American farmer by the name of Christine Pompeo, who grows enough food on a half-acre site in South Portland to supply shares to twenty families. To make food more accessible and affordable, all these distribution efforts made ample use of SNAP and Double Up Food Bucks programs as well as voucher programs for Women, Infants, and Children (WIC) and lower-income seniors.

As Craig sees it, each of these programs, to various degrees, accomplished two things. The first was to reduce harm for those whose lives had been diminished by structural changes in the region's economy or by global events. Not having enough healthy food to eat is clearly harmful; therefore, the first thing a community must do to respond to that problem is provide food, which is what many of the organization's programs do. But the second thing was to provide a systemic response, one that might offer those who are being harmed a pathway out of poverty. To this end, Cultivating Community took over the New Americans Program in 2009 from another nonprofit organization that had been training refugees and immigrants to become the next generation of farmers at a site in Lisbon, Maine, about thirty miles from Portland. The program is in the process of being moved to the sixty-two-acre Hurricane Valley Farm in West Falmouth, only seven miles from Portland. The farm, which was actually created when a 1767 hurricane "cleared the land" by ripping out its trees, is owned by the Falmouth Land Trust. Through a timely intervention, the trust was able to prevent the farm from becoming a housing subdivision by purchasing a conservation easement on the property. It will be used by Cultivating Community to operate its

New Americans farmer training programs and a host of other farming, gardening, food-training, and education efforts.

"We are trying to not *do things to people*," Craig told me. "We want to empower them to start and own their own businesses and to make a contribution to their own community. We can be the gatekeepers, so to speak, by securing resources like land and shaking down USDA for as much money as we can." But like other food nonprofits over the past decade, Cultivating Community is learning that simply producing or distributing more food is not the answer. It has worked with the Portland Food Council to increase the city's minimum wage, and it provides a vital piece to the city's food scene by bringing food production as close as possible to a densely built city. And it reminds the larger community that food may be one of the best ways available to celebrate Portland's growing diversity.

The Rough Beast

But even now, "what rough beast, its hour come round at last, / Slouches towards Bethlehem to be born?" I use the oft-quoted line from W. B. Yeats to circle back to the threat that Portland's foodies can't ignore and that its social workers struggle to control: opioid addiction, the latest tip of the iceberg that may yet sink many ships. As Maine's past collides with its present, food takes us into the lives of people for whom the day-to-day is nothing more than twenty-four hours stretched taut on the rack of life. For most of us, Portland's food scene transports us along a trail of dancing taste buds and scents so deliriously fine that the boundaries between heaven and earth are forever dissolved. But for those at Preble Street, two eggs sunny-side up and a slice or two of non-artisanal toast are not only their best meal—on some occasions, they may be their last.

"Our bathrooms are equipped with motion detectors," Donna Yellen tells me. "If the outside light goes off because the person inside is motionless for thirty seconds, we rush in." She's referring to the horrifying fact that too many of Maine's opioid-addicted residents find themselves overdosing at Preble Street. As much as the center respects the privacy and dignity of its clients, it was forced to cut eighteen inches off the bottoms of its bathroom doors to reduce the possibility of an overdose. Opioids are killing more people than crack cocaine, and at Preble Street, the first thing that new employees learn is how to administer Narcan and chest compressions. When I ask Mark Swann to give me some opioid-related statistics, he says that in Portland, "we used to have one overdose every year; then it was one every two months, then one every two weeks, and now it's one every eight days."

Not to deliberately overplay the local food irony, Mark says that one person died from an overdose last season near the farmers' market Porta-Potty stalls. And in case anyone thinks that class and education steer one away from the dark road of addiction, he tells me that an adjunct professor at the local art school died from an overdose. While the state's former industries were busy fleeing a sinking ship, shortsighted policy makers refused to send lifeboats to those struggling to stay afloat. Lack of public funding for homeless, mental health, and health services meant that not only were the most needy left literally out in the cold, but numerous nonprofit organizations that would ordinarily help them also withered on the vine. According to Mark, seven Portland shelters have closed over the last twelve years. And Maine's notorious two-term Governor Paul LePage has done all he can—he's vetoed funding for Medicaid seven times during his eight years in office—to pour salt in the state's gaping wound.

Mark ticks off a litany of public policy failures that are only now receiving some redress. A loss of medical health insurance through Maine's failure to fund Medicaid and the deinstitutionalization of the mentally ill without supportive outpatient care have both contributed to an ongoing crisis for the state's growing numbers of vulnerable people.

(Fortunately, a 2017 referendum to restore state Medicaid funding passed even though Governor LePage continues to oppose it—he was out of office as of January 2019.) The advocates like Mark, Donna, and the Cumberland County Food Security Council (Portland is in Cumberland County) work in various ways to counter these debilitating trends through legislative advocacy and the expansion of federal food programs. They also persuaded an L.L.Bean matriarch, who was horrified by Maine's high food insecurity rate and wanted to start food banks at Maine's state universities, that her support for federal nutrition program outreach would be more effective. One result of this intervention was that Maine went from having one of the worst Summer Food Service Program participation rates to the nation's sixth highest.

As public awareness about the challenges associated with opioid addiction grows, Mark is optimistic about the prospect of the state's funding a comprehensive prevention initiative. He says they may not get all that they want—he's a realist with an optimistic aura—but feels that it could be a good start. Until real progress is made, however, Preble Street and other agencies are a critical part of a torn safety net that saves far more people than it loses. "We teach our staff to do chest compressions on those who are overdosing," says Donna. "They talk to them and try to bring them back to life. But when that doesn't work, we teach them to say goodbye with love."

Taking Care of Our Own

According to Maine's Good Shepherd Food Bank, Maine is the seventh most food-insecure state in the country. This is a bit of an anomaly, given its location in the Northeast, which as a region generally stays on the better end of the national food security ratings. At the same time, Portland stands out as an oasis, not just because of its dynamic food scene and progressive attitudes but also because people have an unstated tradition of coming together to solve problems. According to Jim Hanna, the director of the Cumberland County Food Security Council, "People here do cooperate, perhaps because we believe that we need to take care of each other. After all, Mainers have an ethic of self-reliance that goes way back." When problems are as complex and deeply rooted as they are in Portland, being a small city can make a difference. Hanna says that "Portland is small enough so that it's easier to get things done, perhaps because everybody knows each other." On a practical note, he adds that "the Maine self-reliance ethic starts with what you have, and when food is what you have to work with, that's where you start to fix things."

Nowhere is the spirit of cooperation more evident than with the Cumberland County Food Security Council. Comprising nearly forty people representing almost the full swath of the city and county's food system, the council embraces a full menu of issues that are both short-term and farsighted. They support Portland's local food scene, but as Jim says, "We celebrate food but not in an elitist fashion." This sentiment finds expression in Portland's farmers' markets, which accept SNAP benefits and also participate in various Double Up Food Bucks and voucher programs. Perhaps the place where the council best embodies its mission is in the public schools with which it is working to conduct a food assessment. The assessment is under way as of this writing but when complete will include a comprehensive review of school gardens, federal nutrition programs (breakfast, lunch, and after school), the health and nutrition curriculum, sustainability and food waste. Given that half of Portland's schoolchildren qualify for free school meals, and that all the city's elementary schools offer a BackPack Program (food sent home with lower-income children for the weekend), the stakes are high. With many children getting almost half their daily nutrition from school meal programs, the council wants to ensure that the schools' nutrition progams are performing optimally.

But like many of the food-oriented programs in Portland (e.g., Cultivating Community), the council doesn't stop with food. It keeps a careful eye as well on city government, continuously holding it accountable for the health and well-being of the community and its people. The food council, for instance, had the mayoral candidates in 2015 lay out their plans for food policy. But it recognizes that the lack of food is not the problem; it's the lack of resources to purchase food that must ultimately be resolved. That's why the council advocates for such initiatives as raising the city's and state's minimum wage as well as other policy efforts designed to address the structural inequities of America's economic system.

There's always much more that can be said about a place like Portland, Maine. There's a young man by the name of Jason Fertig, with whom I was never able to connect but who has a successful fermentation business that numerous millennials I encountered raved about. I could wax ecstatic about the dozen or so raw oysters I feasted on the evening of my birthday that were so sublime I was certain this is the first course they serve you when you enter heaven. I could have explored the mussel farms and other seafood farming operations that hug Casco Bay, but I couldn't find a boat. I could have synthesized the many and wonderful articles found in the *Portland Press Herald*'s Sunday edition in a column called Source, which celebrates the region's nearly endless food scene. I could have documented the food study programs at the University of Southern Maine and the private St. Joseph's College that are both responding to the burgeoning interests of young people in all things food while preparing them for roles as activists, nutrition educators, entrepreneurs, and informed eaters. And, of course, I could have dug deeper into the dark, cold places inhabited by Maine's wounded and injured. But alas, choices had to be made, and my time there was limited.

Portland is a vibrant city and a distinctive food town. It celebrates—indeed, at times revels—in its food scene. But its people, organizations, and government work hard together to ensure that no one is left behind. It is as entrepreneurial a place as you'll ever encounter, but one that serves a triple bottom line of profit, customer, and community. It honors its unique location and traditions, which rest on a rough sea and a rocky soil that have claimed the lives of many Portlanders. In short, Portland is a gem that doesn't conceal its flaws—it just works harder to bring out the radiance in everyone.

Conclusion

In each of the seven cities I visited, I saw people tackling challenges and taking advantage of opportunities in ways that are both common to other US cities and idiosyncratic to their own place. Indeed, even the dichotomy between "challenges" and "opportunities" can sometimes appear murky. One city may be enjoying an influx of millennials and new professional job openings that are driving the demand for better and more diverse kinds of food. Another city may be responding to the need to attract more young people and higher-end jobs by using food as a lure (more restaurants, farmers' markets, and the like). Whether a place views its proverbial glass as half full or half empty, food is fast becoming a necessary part of any social and economic development strategy.

I like to believe that a robust food scene lifts all ships. But I have also seen injustices that run through these seven cities like spiderweb cracks in a windshield. That these communities have hungry residents, people sick from bad diets, divisions that separate black from white from brown, and people dying on their streets is not an indictment of these places as it is an acknowledgment that twenty-first-century America has a long way to go before justice prevails. What is most important, and made obvious in the course of my journeys, is that people are earnestly trying to address these problems—their underlying causes as well as the immediate crisis. While charity is pervasive, the long arc of compassion bends toward justice as we see each community struggle to take care of their own.

The good news is that each city increasingly sees itself as a food system, not just a collection of isolated food programs, services, agencies, and sectors. Yes, like birds, entities of the same feather will flock together. Small food business operators such as processors or restaurateurs look to one another for mutual aid. The nonprofit world hangs out with itself to share information about grants while forming the occasional partnership. Government agencies and elected officials navigate their bureaucracies and governance systems to be responsive to numerous and often competing demands. Collaboration across sectors, however, is occurring, and perhaps most important, awareness of the parts of a local food system, including its regional elements, is becoming more universal. Most of these cities, for instance, either have a food policy council, network, or coalition. (Jacksonville's was recently disbanded, though discussion was under way about reviving it; Boise was kicking the idea around.) Food policy councils and their like build networked approaches to food system issues. As Anne Palmer from the Johns Hopkins Center for a Livable Future puts it, "A lot of social capital is built when people no longer work in isolation."

But what was most interesting and perhaps surprising to me, and what I might consider the top takeaway of this book, was the sheer primacy of individual action, sustained over a significant period of time. Whether we're talking about a for-profit entrepreneur, an elected official, a community organizer, or someone who may rise to the level of visionary, I discovered that the drive and imagination of a relatively small number of people is what's elevating the food scene. This is not individualism in the sense of the "go it alone," self-sufficient, self-made woman or man variety. No. This is the individual who is eager to make things happen, but who *also* seeks out the participation of a wider community.

This conclusion might seem contrary to more democratic models of community development, including ones that this author has espoused. But try as I might, I cannot imagine these communities achieving the success they have without the people I interviewed. Would other people, agencies, market forces, or some yet unimagined exigency have spawned similar results? Perhaps, but for now, I have seen the future of food and community development, and it looks very much like the people revealed in these seven cities. I'll tip my hat to systems, well-managed work teams, and collective impact, but without those necessary kernels of inspiration, instigation, and initiation, the team would never take the field.

What else can be said about these places that might also apply to communities across the United States? In what might be considered the food version of the new normal, all seven communities had farmers' markets, farm-to-table restaurants, brewpubs and microbrews, locally owned coffee shops and roasters, farm-to-school programs (Sitka had a fisherman-to-school program!), food pantries and food banks, food co-ops or some form of a natural food store (or both), food processors and value-added food businesses, a spirit of entrepreneurism, and some kind of organized economic development initiative that included food (e.g., bringing a supermarket to a food desert, supporting new food businesses).

As "local food" has grown over the years, it has often been painted as an elitist offspring—a kind of trust fund baby, if you will—of much wider changes in the food system. Farmers' markets selling organic produce priced higher than anything you'll find at Walmart is one common tagline among those who are allergic to buying something directly from the person who produced it. While this notion may still have currency in some circles, all seven cities had in place at least one significant effort to "democratize and normalize" access to locally produced food for its lower-income residents. Usually this was in the form of Double Up Food Bucks for SNAP recipients, but other incentives or even direct subsidies were also employed to effectively reduce the price of healthy food. In Sitka, for example, the fishermen themselves voluntarily reduced the price of the fish they sold to the schools.

What is perhaps more perplexing is the relationship between some of the trendier food outlets and the cost of housing in nearby neighborhoods. When a new espresso bar opens up, you can almost hear a longtime resident say, "Oh no, there goes the neighborhood!" In what might be a chicken-or-egg question, do we know if more upscale residents move to an area because there are now cooler places to eat, and thus drive up the rents, or do such establishments follow inevitable population migrations, knowing that a new market has now been created, consisting of, say, more millennials? While much more formidable forces—such as a lack of programs to maintain affordable housing, or the appearance and disappearance of certain kinds of higher-wage employers—are generally larger drivers of rents and housing prices, the food movement has the obligation to be sensitive to its own impact on surrounding neighborhoods.

Another important factor, though not always a consistent one, was local government engagement with food issues. There's no substitute for progressive political leadership that supports smart and equitable community development. I emphasize "support" over "lead" because I have found that governments work best when they barely lag behind their citizens rather than trying to be out front, screaming "Follow me!" People and places that seem to have just the right touch are Elaine Clegg and the Boise City Council, and the mayor and the city council of Portland, Maine. The Central Louisiana Economic Development Alliance in Alexandria, the Southeast Alaska Regional Health Consortium in

Sitka, the Community Foundation of the Mahoning Valley, and We Care Jacksonville are good examples of nonprofit institutions stepping up when government is either unwilling or unable to play a strong role. While Bethlehem and Youngstown city governments lag behind the others, leadership from Bethlehem City Councilwoman Olga Negron and Youngstown Mayor Jamael Tito Brown suggest a more proactive response is also emerging in those places.

In any attempt to assign some degree of causality, as I have done with the relationship between food and community vitality, there are always a long list of anomalies, outliers, and other factors to consider. For instance, as with just about every aspect of community life these days, the impact of the millennial population bulge must be accounted for. As the USDA has indicated, "Millennials will be an important driver in the economy for years to come." They demand healthier and fresher food, and they eat out more often. While their presence in my seven cities was not large enough to create a food tsunami comparable to the one that has engulfed Brooklyn, the fact that small numbers were showing up in all these places was a trend that needs to be encouraged by the powers that be. Even when the "explosion" they cause in their respective food scenes is more like a "pop," millennials and those just a little older are causing an outsize ripple when they assume leadership roles as they are doing in Youngstown and elsewhere. The business and social entrepreneurs I met in Jacksonville and Sitka were generally under forty, but their energy and ideas were having an impact far beyond their relatively young years. And when those young people are returning to their hometowns "to make a difference," "to give back," or simply out of some homing instinct, as many of them are, those towns should do everything they can short of a ticker-tape parade to welcome them back.

Another impact, one that does have at least tangential links to food, are major changes in a region's economy. The closing of an auto plant can be a body blow to a place already crippled by deindustrialization. The expansion or location of major new industry sites like those of Amazon can be cause for revelry, at least for some. But I will hold to one overarching economic development principle—that as in nature, diversity is not just better than homogeneity, it's necessary for survival. Whether your economy is on the upswing or slipping into the doldrums, you can't go wrong by paying attention to the many facets of the food system that can add value to a city or region.

By way of illustration, consider the differences between Bethlehem and Youngstown, two former industrial cities that were placed in hospice care when their once mighty steel corporations collapsed like ancient volcanoes. Bethlehem rebounded, first with state support in the form of a casino that attracted much-needed outside consumer dollars and a modicum of culinary class. This gave the city an economic beachhead from which to create a vibrant arts scene, which led in turn to a diverse set of restaurants, farmers' markets, food enterprises, and festivals. While this progression of events is not perfectly linear, it does indicate how baby steps can become giant steps, and how a new advance can feed off a previous one. Youngstown, on the other hand, failed to find anything to plug the hole left by the closing of Youngstown Sheet and Tube. It promptly spiraled downward in the absence of effective local (sometimes corrupt) and state government assistance. In Pennsylvania, the cavalry rode to the rescue with bugles blaring. In Ohio, they couldn't find an old mule or a pennywhistle to help their besieged neighbors.

But what more can food do? After all, how much can we expect from a farmers' market, a coffee shop, or an innovative community farm? By themselves, food projects, businesses, and government services can't do much more than serve their customers, clients, and employees well. Taken collectively, however, their impact on community life is greater than the sum of their parts. Food feeds community, feeds off community, and, indeed, is community. Yet the next bridge to cross—the one that will take food to the land inhabited by the dragons of poverty, racism, and climate change—will be the ultimate test of its mettle.

As we have seen, poverty and racism fester in places like Jacksonville and Alexandria, while opioids drain the life of the user and the resources of the community in Portland. While Boise appeared immune to obvious signs of poverty, hunger, or racism, it exists as an oasis surrounded by rural poverty and environmental degradation that are perpetuated in many cases by industrial agriculture. The city knows that it cannot raise its quality of life without paying attention to those who surround it, a fact it confronts daily in its role as a progressive anomaly in one of the nation's reddest states.

To proclaim that we are stronger together is a durable cliché in times of stress. But when confronting racism, food faces America's roughest beasts. I have little more to offer on the subject other than a faith, maybe itself not much more than a cliché, that food can heal some of society's most painful hurts and mend its angriest rifts. I have seen the beginnings of that stitching together in some of the places I visited as well as in other places I've not included in this book. The potential for closing the racial divide is certainly present, but will require considerably more intentional effort from all parties if it is to succeed. And given the real threats facing all American communities—inequality, climate change, declining human health—success would be strongly advisable.

As we have seen in Jacksonville and Sitka, and to lesser degrees elsewhere, the effects of climate change are becoming more obvious from year to year. In the case of Native Alaskans, climate change threatens their cultural survival. My conversations about climate in the seven cities reminded me of what people said about the connection between diet and health thirty years ago: we know that what we are eating is not good for us, but we're not sure what to do about it. Like those who would eventually modify their individual diets but hadn't yet found their way to collective action—policy changes, healthy-eating incentives, pressure on the food industry—we may try to lower our individual carbon footprints, but we have yet to assemble the public will to make the big, necessary changes. Those conversations are just starting to take place among local food system stakeholders. They must be encouraged so that their participants are emboldened to take more concerted action.

Should, by a bizarre twist of fate, I be elected mayor of a struggling city, I would move ahead aggressively with the following "lessons learned." First, foster a climate of social and economic entrepreneurism. Nurture, nest, and incubate the creative impulse of the people so that a thousand ideas bloom. Even if economic development funds are limited, provide seed grants where possible, and promote forums to raise up ideas, provide technical assistance, and offer mutual support to budding entrepreneurs. Ancillary to this strategy, I would put up the welcome sign for millennials—those who are returning home as well as those who never left. And whatever public "goodies" might be available—first-time homebuyer assistance targeting declining neighborhoods; two-dollar local craft beers every Thursday night on the town green—I would be certain to promote, even if I was the one drawing the beers.

I would pull together my economic development, planning, and public health staff to make food a priority. Were there neighborhoods underserved by affordable and healthy food outlets? They would be the first to receive assistance. Do we know how much food is purchased annually in our city by both the private and public sectors? If not, I would commission the necessary study; once those numbers are known, we would set goals for the purchase of food that is produced, processed, and distributed by locally owned farms and companies. Are there hospitals and educational institutions within my city limits who are not doing all that they can to support our local economy, including buying local food? If they weren't, I would meet frequently with their respective CEOs to ask why not, and if they persisted with bureaucratic mumbo jumbo, invite them to weekly luncheons where I'd serve only locally produced meals until they relented. Of course, the educational institutions would be expected to offer a variety of courses and programs on food and farming; the health care institutions would be expected to make "Food Is Medicine" both a mantra and a policy. Finally, I'd identify the brightest and most enthusiastic member of my staff and appoint her my Minister of Multicultural Celebration and Festivalization. Her sole duty will be to bring merriment to the streets of our city.

I will cast my eyes beyond the city limits and let it be known that all who produce food and beverages for our city are welcome, provided they care for our region's natural resources and the people who work for them. If they can't do that, then they are welcome to change, and I and my administration will do all that we can to help them move in that direction. We'll let it be known that if you are a farmer selling food to us, we will do our part to ensure that your quality of life is not below ours. And if you are already a citizen of our place but struggle to make ends meet or wrestle with addictions, we are ready to ensure a healthy diet, and with assistance from our state and national governments that we will insist upon, the services you need will be provided.

Sustainability will inform all our work, and resilience in the face of climate change will be our manifesto. We will own what we have done to the earth by collectively altering our behaviors and by fighting any action that denies future generations the same well-being that we have enjoyed. I will ride my bike to all public events, carry my groceries in my baskets, and encourage others to do the same. My children and spouse will probably do even more, putting their old man to shame.

And every morning before I head out on my daily mission, I will lift my glasses to my face, the ones specially fitted with equity lenses, so that I can more clearly see the accumulated injustices of the place I was elected to govern. I will let others look through those spectacles as well so that they may see what I do, and that together we can work for the necessary corrections.

There are many other lessons that can be derived from my delightful strolls through the fields and streets of these seven cities. I have chosen to highlight those that rise, in my mind, to the level of universal and, likewise, settle to the level of common denominator. I urge you, reader, to consider all these stories in hopes that you will ferret out the lessons that most resonate with you. But the final lesson comes to me by way of Wendell Berry. Actually, it comes to Wendell Berry by way of the poet William Carlos Williams, whose simple lines adorn this book's front page. In his study of Williams, Berry finds the value of community life comes from the sense of "completeness or fullness" that it affords the person with the imagination to know the limits of desire (e.g., greed, gluttony) and to experience a contentment from an immersion in a place. While Berry and Williams draw on higher artistic sensibilities, their metaphors are decidedly gustatory. As Williams says, "The stomach is full, the ocean no fuller, both have the same quality of fullness. . . . Having eaten, the man has released his mind." And Berry adds, "If we are complete, then we don't have to be limitlessly greedy—and forever disappointed. We don't have to consume the whole creation or burst."

Coming together with the hearts and minds of these poets, and the places and people I visited, I realized how richly you can live off the fruits of your community. And in turn, how satisfying it can be to feed that community, whether it's as directly as producing food or as indirectly as making sure that all have food. Communities may never be entirely "complete"—human invention refuses to be corralled—and our urge for greater abundance will always ignite our imaginations. But knowing that all we need is found within our own boundaries can be an immensely liberating way to live.

Acknowledgments

Setting out on my journey to explore the food systems of seven cities would have been a hopeless if not hapless enterprise without the able assistance of some highly competent and committed guides. Lucky for me, I found eight Beatrices and Virgils to show me the way through the wonders of seven amazing places. My perpetual gratitude goes out to Laureen Husband in Jacksonville, Florida; Karen Schubert in Youngstown, Ohio; Susan Dalandan in Bethlehem, Pennsylvania; John Cotton Dean in Alexandria, Louisiana; Keith Nyitray and Charles Bingham in Sitka, Alaska; Jim Hanna in Portland, Maine; and Eileen Stachowski in Boise, Idaho. I couldn't have done this without all of you!

During the course of my research and especially my visits to these seven cities, I interviewed a total of 92 people and met with another 195 through various focus groups, forums, and workshops. I am grateful to every one of you for your time and insights. Whether your name appears in this book or not, please know that every word you uttered—even the polite silences that sometimes followed my less-than-thoughtful questions—have found their way into this book. I did my best to absorb your perspectives and tried my darnedest to do justice to your ideas.

Bibliography

Berry, Wendell. *The Poetry of William Carlos Williams of Rutherford.* Berkeley, CA: Counterpoint, 2011.

Block, Peter. *Community: The Structure of Belonging.* Oakland, CA: Berrett-Koehler Publishers, Inc., 2008.

Brown, Corie. "Feds won't make good food happen. So cities, armed with food policy councils, will do it themselves." *The New Food Economy,* December 12, 2017. https://newfoodeconomy.org.

Chocano, Carina. "Group Think." *New York Times,* April 22, 2018, 9–11.

Federal Reserve Bank of St. Louis, Board of Governors of the Federal Reserve System. *Harvesting Opportunity: The Power of Regional Food System Investment to Transform Investments.* St. Louis, MO: Self-published, 2017.

Goddard, Summer. "Get Thee to a Brewery." *High Country News,* May 14, 2018, 8.

Gopnik, Adam. "After the Fall." *New Yorker,* February 12, 2018, 92–97.

Hill, David J. "Food Systems Planning Experts Say It's Time to Reflect on Local Governments' Efforts." University at Buffalo (website), October 18, 2018. http://www.buffalo.edu.

Irwin, Neil. "One County Thrives While a Neighbor Struggles." *New York Times*, July 1, 2018, 4.

Kilgannon, Corey. "A Vibrant City's Vacant Look." *New York Times*, September 19, 2018.

Kuhns, Annemarie, and Michelle Saksena. *Food Purchase Decisions of Millennial Households Compared to Other Generations.* EIB-186. Washington, D.C.: United States Department of Agriculture, Economic Research Service, December 2017.

Lee, Matt, and Ted Lee. "Beer Gets Its Own Neighborhood in Charleston." *New York Times*, April 29, 2018.

Phillips, Rhonda, and Robert H. Pittman. *An Introduction to Community Development.* 2nd ed. New York: Routledge, 2015.

Putnam, Robert, and Lewis M. Feldstein. *Better Together: Restoring the American Community.* New York: Simon and Schuster, 2003.

Roberts, Wayne. *Food for City Building: A Field Guide for Planners, Actionists & Entrepreneurs.* Hypenotic Inc., 2014.

Santa Fe Food Policy Council. "Tracking Our Food Economy." Santa Fe, NM: Self-published, 2018. https://www.santafefoodpolicy.org.

Stewart, James B. "A Corporate Behemoth Cometh." *New York Times*, November 16, 2018, B1 and B7.

Wilcox, Meg. "Maine Is Scaling Up Its Local Grain Economy." *Civil Eats*, November 26, 2018.